Vacation days in Greece

Rufus B. Richardson

Alpha Editions

This edition published in 2024

ISBN : 9789362093158

Design and Setting By
Alpha Editions
www.alphaedis.com
Email - info@alphaedis.com

Contents

PREFACE

During a residence of eleven years in Greece I have formed the habit of writing to certain periodicals descriptions of my journeys. The occasion for making a book out of these articles was the suggestion on the part of many members of the American School of Classical Studies, at Athens, who had shared these journeys with me, that I should do so, and so make the descriptions accessible to them. I yielded to this suggestion all the more readily from the consideration that my wanderings have taken me into many nooks and corners not usually visited by those whose stay in the country is short.

Having seen the sunrise from most of the mountain-tops of the country, having forded many of its rivers, and having caught the indescribable color at early dawn and at evening twilight, from the deck of coasting steamers, all along these fascinating shores, I felt it only right that I should try to convey to others, less fortunate than myself, some picture, however inadequate, of all this experience and enjoyment. All that is here set down is, however, but a part of a larger picture that is ever present in my memory.

For the most part I have avoided what has been most frequently described. Athens, Olympia, and the much-visited Argive plain, I have not touched upon, because I did not wish to swell the book by telling thrice-told tales. I tell of what I have most enjoyed, in the hope that readers may feel with me the charm of this poet's land, which has, more than any other, "infinite riches in a little room."

The slight alterations that I have made in the original form of the descriptions was made with the design of bringing them, in a measure, up to the present time. I have also arranged them on a geographical thread, running from the Ionian Islands, through Northern Greece to the Peloponnesus. The two larger articles, on Sicily and Dalmatia, are not simply tacked on. They belong to the subject, inasmuch as Sicily was an important part of Hellas, as the Greeks called their country, and inasmuch as Greek colonies once skirted the greater part of the coast of Dalmatia.

In regard to the spelling of proper names, I have tried to shun unusual appearances. But I have great objection to changing all the Greek endings in *os* into *us*, just because the Romans did so. I also object to changing the Greek *k* into *c* where it will surely be pronounced as an *s*. In the case of names that have become a part of our English speech, I have, however, admitted these changes. The result may not seem satisfactory, on account of the lack of a rigid system; but I trust that it will be pardoned.

CORFU

It is great good fortune to spend a week in Corfu on the way to Greece. Seeing it from one end to the other, wandering through its olive forests and vineyards, brings on a mild, or, in some cases, a wild, intoxication without wine. What words fit the surrounding beauty but "Islands of the Blessed," "Elysium," "Garden of Eden," "Paradise"? It is not Heaven, after all, for one sees here the poor, lame, blind, begging for small alms; but, as long as earth holds such corners as Corfu, it is not all cursed.

To the traveller who has felt the intoxication of such a region, and is impelled to report something of it, the impotence of words comes home with special force. Naught but the painter's art seems adequate to report Corfu. And, furthermore, painter as well as poet might here well feel the weakness of his art. It is a great boon to have had this realm of beauty brought upon the retina of the eye, and so communicated to the soul.

One may, perhaps, be allowed to group the impressions that Corfu makes, and report them with a plainness that aspires only to the office of a photograph, resigning the attempt at coloring.

Before the eye lies one Corfu—the Corfu of to-day; but before the mind are brought two others—the Kerkyra of Greek history and the Scheria of Homer. The two latter compete with the former, and refuse the present beautiful scene a monopoly of attention.

But, first, to be just to the present Corfu. The traveller who has never been east of Italy, which was my case at the time of my first visit in 1890, feels that he is here passing for the first time the bounds between Europe and the Orient. The streets and squares of the city, which contains a population of about 30,000—about one-third of the population of the whole island— swarm with figures clad in the most wonderful costumes, men and women vying with one another in display of colors. The Corfiotes themselves contribute largely to this display of costumes. From across the narrow strait come from Epirus many Albanians, with their big white skirts and their kingly air, some for trade and a quick return, and some for a longer stay. From the same quarter come the no less picturesque people, partly Greek and partly Wallachian—but who can give the component parts of the blood of these people of Epirus?—who, having attempted to secure the consummation of what the Congress of Berlin decreed, incorporation with Greece, were treated as Turks usually treat insurgents, and were then living as refugees in Corfu, awaiting the hour when Moslem rule shall recede from the shores of Europe. Some of these men's costumes are ragged and dirty, but with what an air the men walk in them. It is not a swagger, but a king's gait. A well-dressed European gentleman can as little compete with these men for attention as the Berlin palace can compete with the picturesque ruins of Heidelberg. The clergy, who seem numerous enough here to preach the Gospel to every creature, with their long black gowns and high stiff caps, make quite a feature in the throng. The military officers are also numerous and brilliantly dressed, but are too much like ordinary Europeans to attract particular notice.

The vegetation here is also Oriental—oranges, lemons, figs, forests of cactus and giant aloes abound. The four or five million olive-trees, many sixty feet high, are the characteristic features of the island. They form a beautiful background for the tall, dark-green cypresses. But the vine presses hard upon the olive. It is great good fortune to be here in the time of the grape harvest, even if one must miss the oranges and the olives. One day in September I walked to Palæokastritza, an old cloister on a rock looking out on the Ionian Sea, sixteen miles from the city. The way was through a continuous vineyard full of laborers. At this season of the year there is hardly a drop of running water in the island. There are places where springs and brooks and even rivers have been and will be again, but there are none there now. The water in the wells and cisterns looks suspicious. But one has a substitute for water that is just about as cheap. For copper coin of the value of two cents a woman gave me a pile of grape clusters, enough for four men. On my return I managed to signify with my poor Greek to a man riding on a load of grapes that I would like to change places with him. For three miles I rode stretched out on the top of crates full of grapes, resting my tired feet, eating, by the permission of the driver, from the top of the crates, while from the bottom the precious juice oozed out and trickled into the dusty road. I felt that I was playing Dionysos. Then it was that the vintagers, many women and few men, came trooping picturesquely from the fields. They looked so happy that it seemed as if the contagion of joy rested in the vine. It seemed as if a touch of music would have converted them into a Dionysiac chorus.

If Corfu had no classical history, it would still be historically interesting. It has been spared that curse which rested so long on the rest of Greece—Turkish occupation. The Turks dashed their forces in vain in two memorable sieges against its rock forts. The high degree of culture here, as compared with the rest of Greece, outside of Athens, is partly due to this exemption. But there have been stimulating influences from without. Rome, Byzantium, Naples, Venice, and England have held sway here. The rule of Venice, to which the Corfiotes gave themselves voluntarily, as they had formerly done to Rome, lasted nearly six hundred years, with the interruption of the Anjou episode. This rule was mild and beneficent. It was the Venetians who built the fortifications which kept off the Turks, and which still form, though to a less degree than twenty-five years ago, the characteristic feature in the aspect of the city.

From Waterloo to 1864 England exercised a protectorate over this and the six other Ionian Islands. Ten successive Lord High Commissioners, of whom Gladstone was one, and whose monuments profusely deck the esplanade, represented here the majesty of England. The English built the present fine system of roads—paid for, of course, in Ionian money. A kindly feeling prevails toward England because she yielded to the strong desire of the inhabitants for union with the kingdom of Greece. But the fact that the English, on their departure, blew up the principal fortification of the harbor on the island Vido, and carried away all the guns from the other forts, left a sting. The dismantled fort was paid for in Ionian money, but the exigencies of European politics demanded the dismantling. Austria had as much to say about that as England. But, sweeping away the name of Corfu, which arose in the Middle Ages, and transferring ourselves back of all this foreign occupation and centuries of semi-barbarism, let us introduce ourselves to the Greek Kerkyra of Thucydides. Passing southward, a half a mile or so from the esplanade of the present city, one comes along an isthmus between two old harbors to an elevated peninsula, on which now stands the King's villa in a beautiful garden. Here one is overpowered by historic associations. Here lay the proud Greek colony established by Corinth in 734 B.C., a colony that first set the example of filial ingratitude, and, feeling itself stronger than the mother city, joined battle with her and defeated her in the first great naval battle of Greeks against Greeks, in 665 B.C. From this rising ground the eye dimly discerns in the distance, near the mainland opposite the southern end of the island, the Sybota Islands, where the later great naval battle between mother city and colony in the presence of an Athenian fleet gave the occasion for the dreadful Peloponnesian war. From this inner harbor, now abandoned and still, nearly silted up and yearly submitting to the encroachment of vines upon its borders, the proud fleet of Alcibiades and Nicias sailed for Syracuse. It was the alliance with Kerkyra, the key to the voyage to Sicily, that lured the Athenians to that ruin.

Little of this Kerkyra remains above ground. Perhaps much may yet be found below. About twelve years ago excavations by Carapanos laid bare a great quantity of terra-cottas. Perhaps it was a terra-cotta manufactory that he discovered. The ruins of an old Doric temple lie on the surface of the ground near a spring in an olive grove on the side of the peninsula looking toward the mainland. The situation, 100 feet above the strait, among the olives and near an ancient fountain, makes one feel that he could have joined in doing honor to the dryads and naiads with the throng that used to meet here. One of the antiquarians of Corfu has lately advanced the view that these remains are those not of a temple but of a bath. Blessed bathers!

It was not bad taste for the King of Greece to put his gardens on the spot of the Gardens of Alkinoos. If I were King of Greece I would try to compound with my subjects to take the business of ruling off my hands and let me keep my Corfu home. It is no wonder that Elizabeth, the Empress of Austria, sought relief from her troubles in her villa on the other side of the inner harbor.

When a part of the Venetian works was being removed in 1843, where the isthmus between the two old harbors joins the present city, there was found a circular monument about twenty feet in diameter, ending in a flat cone, and containing an inscription running almost around the layer of stones just below the coping. It reads thus: "This is the monument of Menekrates, son of Tlasias, of Œantheia by birth. The people erected it in his memory, "for he served them well as *proxenos*" (consul) "and he perished in the sea." This with more, making six hexameters, now much more obscured than when first discovered and copied, I made out by the help of a manual of epigraphy in the rays of the sun just rising over the mountains of Epirus. The archaic forms of the letters make it a remarkable inscription, which may be dated as far back as 600 B. C. As I read this inscription, a century older than the Persian war, and two centuries before Thucydides, I thought, here surely one is in contact with Greek antiquity.

The next day, in an upper room of the building used for both library and high school, in company with the director, Professor Romanos, and Professor Papageorgios, a gentleman who deserves the title *philoxenos*, I read the other inscriptions of Corfu which have not been lost in the labyrinths of the British Museum or elsewhere. Some of these are of about the same age as that on the Menekrates monument, but very clear as well as exceedingly interesting on account of the old forms of the letters. They are mostly tomb inscriptions, telling of the grief which all the world has felt over the loss of the brave and the good.

CORFU. MOUTH OF THE OLD HARBOR WITH "SHIP OF ULYSSES"

One need not linger too long over Kerkyra. It is a state which we cannot love. We cannot forget that before Salamis it held its fleet off the southern point of the Peloponnesus, waiting to see which way the great struggle was going to incline. When Athens concluded the alliance with her at the opening of the Peloponnesian war, many at Athens felt it to be an unholy alliance, and that the burden of hatred thus shouldered was almost a counterbalance to the winning of the second navy in Greece. Thucydides draws an awful picture of the decimating feuds, which seemed tinged with barbaric fury, between aristocracy and commons. In his pages the island vanishes from view bathed in blood.

Long before the time of Thucydides the natives of this island stoutly maintained their descent from the oar-loving Phæacians of Homer. Their land was Scheria, the home of Alkinoos. This belief, in which they took so much pride, really made them great as a naval power; and he who would to-day take away the charm of Homeric tradition from this land, which has been made by it into holy ground, would work it a greater injury than one who should despoil it of its olive-trees. Of course, our enjoyment of Homer does not depend on localizing his story:

"Was sich nie und nirgends hat begeben

Das allein veraltet nie."

And yet the story of the Odyssey, localized here from gray antiquity, one likes, while here, to believe; to read as if there had been nobody to bring up any objections to its geography, or to reason about its geography at all—to read it, in short, with Corfiote eyes and Corfiote fancy.

Does not the very ship which Poseidon turned into stone, because it conveyed Ulysses home, still stand at the mouth of the old inner harbor? Yesterday I passed the bridge over the Potamo, where, according to Gregorovius, Ulysses was cast ashore, and tumbled out of the stream that had received him to sink exhausted in his long sleep under the double tree. I can almost go farther here than I am asked to go. Methinks that under yonder tree, which looks as if it might count almost any number of centuries, the sturdy swimmer fell asleep and awoke so sweetly. It does not matter that another place near the entrance of the old harbor has come to honor in the mouths of the natives as the spot of the meeting between Ulysses and Nausikaa. Our mood adapts itself kindly to either locality. Somewhere hereabouts we will let the sweet story have a local habitation. Let fancy for the hour hold sway. Thus we are perchance brought nearer to the clever voyager, the beautiful maid, the garrulous old king guided by his wife in the midst of his sailor people. Ah! the fiction of Homer holds the mind in more abiding thrall than the facts of Thucydides.

A DAY IN ITHACA

Ithaca was the first of the great Homeric places of renown to "swim into my ken," if it can be said to have swum into my ken when I saw it by the light of the full moon in sailing from Corfu to Patras. But I became acquainted with Troy and Mycenæ long before I really appropriated Ithaca. This I got by the method of gradual approach, a method which has a certain charm only granted to one who is privileged to reside a series of years near his goal.

On a journey to Dodona, the year after this moonlight view, our steamer, in passing from Patras to Prevesa, put in at Bathy, officially called Ithaca, on the east side of the island; and I had just one hour ashore which was more tantalizing than satisfactory as far as studying the topography of Ithaca was concerned; and yet one may believe that he sees in the beautiful bay and harbor the very harbor of Phorkys, where Ulysses landed after his twenty years' absence. The cave of the Nymphs, where the jolly Phæacians laid him asleep with his treasures about him was not visible; but we were told that this is now farther up the hill.

After an interval of several years, in which I had passed Ithaca several times in the night, I set foot on it again in a more satisfactory fashion. Taking refuge from the August heat of Athens in the Ionian Islands, I was spending a few days in Argostoli, the chief town of Kephallenia, and seized this opportunity to approach Ithaca from the back side, so to speak. A drive of four hours brought us clear across from the west side of Kephallenia to Samos on the east side, over the high backbone of the island. During the last hour of the journey, the descent, as "the sun was setting, and all the ways were growing shady," our eyes were fastened upon Ithaca lying peacefully in the bosom of Kephallenia—a beautiful sight.

As we had planned for only one day in Ithaca, we determined to make it a long one, and started from Samos in a sail-boat at half-past two in the morning; but, although the sail was filled most of the time, so gentle was the breeze that, even supplemented by the work of the oars, it did not bring us to Ithaca until half-past five. My boy of twelve years, companion of many of my wanderings in Greece, was asleep most of the way, but broke the parallel with Ulysses by waking up when the keel touched the shore.

We landed at the foot of Mount Aëtos, on the top of which Gell and Schliemann place the city of Ulysses, but deferred climbing this until we might see whether our time and strength held out, and pushed at once for our main goal, some ruins near Stauros, at the northern end of the island, nine or ten miles distant. We followed all the way, with an occasional cut-off, the fine carriage road made by the English, to whose occupation the Ionian Islands owe most of their good roads, notably the one on which we had crossed from Argostoli to Samos, which required much difficult and expensive engineering. The road crossed the backbone of Ithaca twice at points where this is somewhat low; but in the last seven miles it followed the western shore about half way up the steep slope which runs down into the sea, leaving almost no strip of level coast. In fact, Ithaca smiles in very few spots, being nearly all mountain, just the country to get attached to. Ulysses naturally enough calls it "rugged, but a good bringer-up of boys," and adds: "I never could find anything sweeter than my native land." In one respect it is doubtless somewhat changed. As we passed along the foot of the principal mountain of the island, a bare height of over 2,600 feet, I asked a peasant its name, and was glad to hear him answer "Neriton." But this is now as undeserving of its constant Homeric epithet of "leaf-shaking" as is Zakynthos of its epithet of "woody." The denudation of the Greek mountains is a sad theme, and is most strikingly illustrated in the Ionian Islands. Mount Aenos, over 5,000 feet high, on Kephallenia, had until about the beginning of the present century its slopes covered with large pines, which were known in all the world as *Abies cephalonica*. But at that time a destructive fire swept away nearly half of this treasure; and two years ago about one-third of the remainder went in the same way. What has occurred here goes on every summer all over Greece; but the loss is in no case so conspicuous as in this. I have seen Pentelicus burning for three days—a brilliant illumination for Athens—and, in sailing from Poros to Nauplia in midsummer, I counted twenty-six fires on the mountains of Peloponnesus; but all these could do nothing more in the way of damage than to help on a little the aridity into which Attica and the Argolid are helplessly sinking. Where it scarcely ever rains during six months of the year, the grass and weeds become like tinder, and a fire once started from some shepherd's carelessness is difficult to stop.

Water was rather scanty on our road, and what we got came from cisterns. Springs are, indeed, rare in Ithaca. But when we came to the famous spring Melanhydro (Blackwater), near Stauros, in the hope of finding something fine, we found the water not only warm, but having three-quarters of a very ripe tomato in it, as well as pieces of a big cactus stalk, and rather full of little pollywogs besides. The proper care of springs is something which the Greeks do not seem to appreciate. I have seen the famous spring Pirene on Acro-Corinth treated even worse than this.

But if the water which we needed for our eighteen-mile walk in the August sun was bad, we found consolation in grapes. I suspect, though I cannot verify it from actual weighing, that my regular allowance of grapes in an August or September day's walk in Greece is ten pounds. One rarely pays anything for these, inasmuch as they are much cheaper than New England huckleberries. While it is considered *contra bonos mores* to take them without asking, peasants seem always glad to give them. On the hottest part of the return journey, as we stopped at a house and asked for grapes, the man of the house said that his vineyard was two kilometres distant, but insisted upon going to it at once. This I could not allow, whereupon, in spite of my protests, he got upon the very top round of a rickety ladder, leaning against the wall of his house, and, at the risk of his neck, pulled down from a vine running over a high trellis two clusters which he feared were not ripe, as proved to be the case. In the meantime his wife had been with great difficulty restrained from setting before us eggs, bread, and cheese, which we refused on the ground that we had just eaten. To be strictly truthful, I ought to state that, not being enough used to the Greek language to discriminate fine shades of meaning, I am not sure but that the man meant to send his wife the two kilometres in question. Greek custom would incline me to this supposition.

Although Ithaca is noted for its hospitality, this treatment is not mentioned as an isolated, but as a typical case of Greek hospitality. I doubt whether there is any people so hospitable as the Greek. The longer I live here and the more I travel about, the more I am impressed with this hospitality. It is not only on this rugged island where men live by "wresting little dues of wheat and wine and oil," "an ill-used race of men," one might be tempted to call them, that the stranger at the gate must come in and have the best that the house affords; at Platæa, six years ago one November night, a house-holder received the American School at Athens, carrying more mud on their persons than it is often the lot of four men to carry, into the only room in his house which had a fire, turning out his family, who were evidently enjoying it, to pass the night in a colder room. And they seemed to take it as a matter of course.

But I have wandered from our goal. I had expected to find in the remains near Stauros corroboration of my belief that here lay the Homeric city. For I had long supposed, with Leake of the older topographers, and Bursian, Partsch, and Lolling of the later ones, that it must be here. Here are massive walls, rock-cut steps, ancient cisterns, and the niches in the rock passing under the name of the "School of Homer." But at the close of the day, in order not to be unjust to the dissenters, I climbed Aëtos, and saw that the walls there, resembling those of Tiryns, had about as good claim as those at Stauros to be regarded as those of a Homeric fortress. The question where the Odyssey locates the city is not at present to be decided by remains, but by certain other indications which seem to point to the region of Stauros.

The suitors of Penelope, who wished to kill Telemachus on his return from "Sandy Pylos," lay in wait for him on an island called Asteris, "midway between Ithaca and rugged Samos." Opposite the northern end of the island, though much nearer to Samos (Kephallenia) than to Ithaca, is the only island in the whole strait, needing to be magnified a good deal to suit the story of the Odyssey; but what poet ever denied himself the right to magnify? And looking toward this little island is the only harbor on this (western) side of Ithaca, a deep indentation running far into the land, now called "Polis Bay," a reminiscence of the fact that a city once stood here. This name is a genuine survival from old times, and not a revamping of a classical name, as is the case with Mount Neriton. About this bay and up as far as Stauros, and even farther to the west and north, is the main smiling spot of the island. It was autopsy that I wanted more than anything else; and, as I stood on the rocks near Homer's school, autopsy forced upon me the conviction that here, and here only, must have been the important city of the island, the city from which the faithful Paladin of Agamemnon ruled not only Ithaca but also Kephallenia. Here, amid the remains of an ancient settlement, one looks into three harbors about equally distant, Polis on the west side of the island, a broader one on the east side, now called Phrikes, in which we saw a good-sized vessel anchored, and on the north end one still more capacious, probably the Reithron of the Odyssey. The situation was well adapted to a city ruling the island and possessing easy communication with the coast, east and west.

ITHACA. POLIS BAY FROM THE NORTH

It is not so very many years ago that general scepticism prevailed about Homeric topography. But now, just as one smiles, in listening to Dörpfeld's masterly exposition of the thoroughly excavated walls of Troy, at the thought that "if Troy ever stood" was catalogued by an almost contemporary poet with insoluble riddles, like "if Israel's missing tribes found refuge here," so, in passing over Ithaca with the Odyssey in hand, one smiles to think that not long ago Hercher could maintain that there was no agreement between the Ithaca of the Odyssey and the Ithaca of reality. It may be granted that Hercher knocked out the somewhat visionary Gell; but he did not touch Leake; indeed, it seems as if he had not read Leake at all. There is one passage in the Odyssey which seemed to support Hercher, in which Ithaca is spoken of as "a low island," and as "lying apart and farther to the west than Samos and Zakynthos." How the poet, be he the original poet of the Odyssey or an *epigonos*, ever happened to say this of Ithaca, the rugged island lying close up against the eastern shore of Kephallenia, no one has yet satisfactorily explained. But, apart from this Homeric crux, there is a most gratifying coincidence between "the Land and the Book." The topography of Ithaca has gained respect in proportion as attempts have been given up to force Corfu into identity with the land of the Phæacians.

In respect to Schliemann's and Gell's acropolis on Mt. Aëtos at the narrowest part of the island, it must be granted that this was an important fortress of the Homeric period, controlling communication between the northern and southern halves of the island, as well as the nearest approach from Samos, which was probably always in antiquity the main city of Kephallenia. But that the main city of Ithaca was ever on this eagle's eyrie is in accordance neither with antecedent probability nor with the poet's story.

It is curious to see how different have been the estimates of the height of this mountain, according as one wished to make it the site of the Homeric Ithaca or not. And, indeed, the figures given in different books which might be supposed to rest on measurements vary also. Probably the figures given by Partsch, 380 metres, are correct. This would make the top about 1,200 feet above the sea level, but only about half that above the high ground over which the road from Bathy passes to the mooring place—it can hardly be called a harbor—opposite Samos. Partsch makes merry at "those whose faith can not only remove mountains, but also make them lower than they actually are, and who speak of the run up the steep sides of Aëtos as if it were only a matter of half an hour." I was in my turn amused to find that in my eagerness to go up this height and down again as soon as possible, in order to take our boat back to Samos, I had made the ascent in considerably less than half an hour. Perhaps the fleet-footed shepherd boy who led me up may have taken me along a good deal faster than Partsch would have gone making his way alone. He ought, however, to have looked out not to spoil a good case by underrating the powers of English pedestrians.

At half-past three we reached the shore, where our boat was tied by the stern cables waiting for us, and we set sail for Samos in such a splendid breeze from the north which had just sprung up, right on our quarter, that no Homeric ship ever sped over the waters with more life than ours. In just one hour and five minutes we landed in Samos, in time for me, though tired, to wander before dark over the high hills containing the acropolis of Samos, the remaining walls of which are most impressive.

The next morning, starting with a carriage at half-past three, we were at eight o'clock in Argostoli. During the slow ascent I kept my eyes fastened upon Ithaca every moment when it was possible to do so. I wanted to see the sunlight once more illumine that long chain of four separate peaks stretched out in the sea from north to south; but before sunrise we had already got into the gorge through which the road pushes up to the top. Our first sight of the island was in the evening twilight and our last in the morning twilight. As I thought it over afterward I could not help thinking that there was an especial propriety in this; for was not Ithaca pre-eminently a land of twilight?

> NOTE.—Since excavating near Stauros in 1901 without finding any Mycenæan remains, Professor Dörpfeld has come to the conclusion that the true Homeric Ithaca was the Island of Leukas, that there was a grand confusing of names prior to Strabo, so that what was really the Homeric Same is now called Ithaca, and what was really Dulichion is now called Kephallenia. Something like this had been previously suggested in order to find a place for the Homeric Dulichion, and also to place Ithaca where it would lie "farthest out to the darkness" and "apart from the other islands." In these two points Homer's geography has never been quite satisfactory, but it is doubtful whether we shall get any revision of it which will be entirely satisfactory. It is possible that the results of Professor Dörpfeld's excavations on Leukas may bring to light such Mycenæan remains as to make the scale tip in his favor. One point in his contention seems certain, viz., that Leukas is geologically an island, and as such should have found a place in the Homeric naming. But the whole question is *adhuc sub judice.*

DELPHI, THE SANCTUARY OF GREECE

After a glorious day spent at Acro-Corinth, the American School, four persons, set out on November 5, 1890, for a ten days' trip through Central Greece. The first point of interest was Delphi.

As, in entrance into some fraternities, a rough and ridiculous initiation increases the pleasure of membership, so in the present case, perhaps, the rough and ridiculous approach to Delphi only served to increase the appreciation of the glory there.

The little Greek steamer which coasts the Corinthian Gulf lay at anchor at Corinth, ready to start at 5 P.M. But though it was so near that one could throw a stone into it from the shore, we paid a drachma and a half apiece for being rowed on board. The boatman got well paid for the few strokes which it took him to cover that short distance.

We paid more than we ought. We had committed the fatal error of asking the price instead of coolly jumping into the boat and paying half a drachma apiece when we reached the steamer. All that we lacked was a little knowledge of the country, the language, the people, and, more than all, the prices. We were paying for our tuition. Six months later, when I was much better informed, I was passing Chalkis, and thought I would like to go ashore for an hour or so. I then asked the boatman, by way of testing him, what he would charge to take me ashore and bring me back again. He replied, "Six drachmas." I laughed, and said, "Half a drachma." "All right," said he, "jump in." When one "knows the ropes" the boatmen are very tractable; but the stranger is at their mercy, because nowhere in Greece, not even at Piræus or Patras, is there a pier for a steamer to tie up to. All this seems managed in the interest of the boatmen.

After ascertaining that we should have to disembark at a very early hour the next morning at Itea, the ancient Chaleion, the port of Delphi (the ticket agent said five o'clock, and the steward of the boat said three o'clock), we all selected state-rooms with care, undressed and went to bed at the early hour of seven, with instructions to the steward to wake us half an hour before the time of disembarkation. Sound slumber, which comes to men wearied with tramping, often makes hours seem short; but, when we were waked, it seemed incredible that we could have had the night's sleep that we had so carefully planned. Our watches soon gave the dreadful corroboration to our suspicions. It was only nine o'clock in the evening.

The boat had skipped Antikyra, shortening the journey by several hours, and was going to stop only half an hour before passing over to Galaxidhi, the ancient Oeantheia. In all my experience in Greece there was only one other case of a steamer being *ahead* of time. But oh! the hours both day and night that I have spent waiting for belated steamers; and no inconsiderable part of these hours has been spent at Itea. Three times, after patience had failed, I have taken a sail-boat across to the Peloponnesian shore, to strike the more regular communication by rail.

When we were fairly landed, the ridiculous part of our initiation was completed, and the rough part began. I would fain pass over that night in the hotel at Itea. It was no worse, however, than almost any night that the traveller passes in places called by courtesy hotels in the country towns of Greece.

Itea, after being for years the despair of travellers, received, as a result of the increased travel brought about by the excavation of Delphi, two very good lodging-houses, and, instead of being known as cheap and nasty, it became a place where one could be fleeced in good style.

The next morning we proceeded a mile or more along the shore to the east, until we identified the ruins of the ancient port of Delphi, Kirrha, which, we are told, the Amphictyons twice destroyed in a rage, though it seems quite un-Greek to do so unreasonable a thing as to destroy the harbor through which one must continue to land. Leaving Kirrha, and putting ourselves about on the track of the old visitors of the holy place of Delphi, who came from Peloponnesus, we passed through miles of the finest olive orchard in Greece to the site of the ancient Krissa at the head of the plain, the old Homeric town which appears to have yielded reluctantly to rising Delphi the control of this region. After the joy of the plain came the joy of climbing the rugged rocks for hours until it seemed as if Delphi must be in the clouds. This double reward for the double initiation suddenly ended when, turning a sharp spur of rock, we found ourselves in the grand natural theatre which was Delphi. Even to one who had never read of it, and did not know what it was to the Greeks, the mere sight of the place must still be one of the finest views in the world. But to one who has come to look on the sanctuary of ancient Greece it is this and more also. The Phædriadæ, which rise sheer behind the wretched village of Kastri, shutting out the higher snow-clad Parnassus from view, seem like no earthly rocks. The Pleistos seems like no earthly river, as it murmurs far below, as if about to tell the sea that it had passed Delphi. Mount Kirphis, fronting the Phædriadæ, and closing the great theatre, seems privileged to have been allowed to stand silently gazing on all that went on in that holy place, and to have been its appointed warder, shutting it in from the eyes of all who would not struggle up here through the mountain passes.

But from reverie to fact the little village of Kastri rudely recalls us. Villagers inform us of a "*megale catastrophe.*" Two nights before, at midnight, a mountain torrent had come down over the Phædriadæ, tearing through the village, sweeping away two of the miserable houses, and rendering several of the adjacent ones unsafe. One child was killed, and everybody thoroughly frightened.

All inquired anxiously whether there was not a chance of the village being soon purchased for purposes of excavation. Visitors from the neighboring town of Arachova, who seemed happy that they were not living in Kastri, said that probably many Kastriots would soon leave their homes anyway, and move to Arachova.

The most important thing in Delphi was, of course, the temple of Apollo, in which was the oracular chasm, influences from which controlled Greece so long. Fragments of the temple lay all around, near and in the houses built above its ancient floor. This floor was so near the surface of the soil that one saw quite a portion of it. By digging away a few feet of earth in one place, an opening was laid bare, by which one could pass down into a series of vaults beneath this floor. Pomtow, who visited Delphi in 1884, counted himself as the third man who had ever crawled in through these vaults. But the exploit subsequently became so common that a fixed price of twelve drachmas was allowed workmen for removing the earth. Perhaps a hundred persons have undergone this crawling process, from which one came out covered with dirt from head to foot, but satisfied that he has seen all that was to be seen of the world-renowned temple.

The village school was a striking sight. Attracted by a loud buzzing sound near the house of the keeper of antiquities, with whom we lodged, we ventured in at the open door whence the sound proceeded, and found about forty boys apparently repeating something after the teacher, who, clad somewhat like the shepherd in the play of "Œdipus," as given at Harvard University, looked like anything but a learned man. He proved to be a gentleman, however, in spite of his rough mantle. After school we ventured with him into his house, from which his family had fled, because a river of mud had flowed through the cellar, and left the walls in a tottering condition. He seemed to possess but little, and yet he took down from the rafters a cluster or two of half-dried grapes, and gave them to us, exhibiting the time-honored Greek hospitality.

But to return a moment to the school. No sooner had we arrived than a dead silence fell upon the crowd. The boys took seats on the long benches resting on the bare earth, and reading of Herodotus in modern Greek began. The first boy, with a voice pitched as high as a steam whistle of small dimensions and high pressure, started off to see how much he could read in a given time. If he saw a period coming, he would catch for breath, and dash over it like a locomotive putting on extra steam to take an up grade. To our utter amazement, the next boy beat the first both in pitch and rapidity. The teacher, without a word, watched the process with apparently rising satisfaction. Meanwhile a boy passed to and fro in the front benches, keeping things wonderfully quiet by striking the ears of the smaller boys with a little twig.

No sooner had we returned to our quarters on our first evening in Delphi, and begun to read the register of people who had visited the house in the past, than, just as we were noticing the name of Bayard Taylor, a peal of thunder reverberated through the great gorge, followed by peal on peal, with rain and lightning, lasting nearly all night. It was so impressive that we wished to expose ourselves to the rain in order the better to see and hear. A sheltering roof, however, was the best place from which to enjoy the storm as much as was possible while disturbed by thoughts of the poor villagers, exposed to further sufferings and fears. He who has not seen Delphi in a thunder-storm has not seen it in all its majesty. It seems made for such spectacles.

The excavations inaugurated by the French School at Athens, soon after our visit, have changed the aspect of Delphi in many respects. As the work has proceeded, I have made annual pilgrimages thither. While one finds the results of intense interest, and sees each year some additional important building brought to light, temple upon temple, the theatre, the stadion, the numerous treasuries of the different cities of Greece with their sculptured adornment, it is still the place itself that impresses one most of all. If one walks through the ruins just at night-fall, one need not ask why the Greeks considered this spot sacred. It is in itself "an awful place." Olympia lies in a charming sunny valley. It was as appropriate to the brilliant games that were held there as was Delphi to the deep religious transactions and the awful oracle that spoke the doom of men and states. There were games at Delphi, as there was religion at Olympia; but at Olympia the games became at least as prominent as the worship of Father Zeus, while at Delphi it was always religion that was paramount.

It would be contrary to the plan of this book to describe in full the excavations of Delphi. It may be said that the results were in some ways disappointing to some people. From certain passages in ancient authors sprung a belief that statues in Delphi might be as "thick as hops." The five hundred bronze statues that Nero is said to have carried away must have made only a small hole in the total number of seventy-three thousand reported by Pliny to have been still remaining in his time. Even if one suspects an error in the text, we know that Demetrios of Phaleron, who passed for a fairly modest man, had three hundred and sixty statues erected to him at Athens during the short time in which he directed the affairs of Athens. And taking this as a sample of the way statues multiplied, we can the more readily swallow Pliny's numerals. At any rate, Delphi is classed by him with Olympia and Athens as the third of the places where statues most abounded. But, for many years after Pliny's time, Delphi doubtless lay open to plunder. The bronzes were melted up and the marbles made into lime.

The yield of statues from the excavations has, it is true, been smaller than many expected it to be. But it would be most absurd to say that the work has been disappointing. The bronze charioteer alone, probably a subsidiary figure in the group dedicated by a member of the Syracusan family, Gelon, Hieron, Polyzalos, would have set the stamp of success upon the enterprise. And, apart from this, there is a whole museum full of statuary of the utmost importance in the history of sculpture. Tombs of the Mycenæan period with rich contents have also added to the interest of the excavations, more important in some aspects than those of Olympia. It will be years before the enormous quantity of inscriptions can be published.

The French excavators are to be congratulated upon the ease with which they got rid of their earth. Their dumping-cars were easily brought to the edge of the gorge of the Pleistos, and the contents shot down thousands of feet, never to trouble them more. How I have envied them when working at Corinth, where one of the chief difficulties has been to find a proper dumping-place for the enormous deposit of from twenty to thirty feet of earth. At Olympia, also, the brook Kladeos was very serviceable in carrying off the dump. It is a pity that one cannot always find an excavation site close by a serviceable river.

DODONA

My friend, Mr. Arthur Hill, the British Vice Consul at Piræus, being about to make a business trip through Epiros in the spring of 1891, invited me to join him. Without this invitation I should have travelled Greece very unsymmetrically, leaving out all the country west of the great Pindos range. It is fair to call this Greece, although, in defiance of the arrangements of the treaty of Berlin, most of it remains politically Turkish.

At Patras we took a little Greek coasting steamer late at night, and, with only one incident worth mentioning, arrived a little after noon the next day at Prevesa on Turkish territory. The one incident was a stop of an hour in the wonderfully retired harbor on the east coast of Ithaca. If Homer had this in mind in describing the harbor of Phorkys he might well say that the ships needed no cable there. Even half an hour on shore for a short Homeric reverie was something to be thankful for. On our boat was a man who looked for all the world like the weather-beaten Ulysses returning from his twenty-years' absence. To my disgust he did not get off at Ithaca to hunt up Penelope, but went on to Leukas.

Arrived in Prevesa, I was made aware that we were off the beaten track by being informed that a letter which I had hastily written to send back to Athens would not even start for six days. This impression was deepened by the information that the British Consul at Prevesa had, during the seventeen years of his sojourn there, never thought of going to Joannina, two days into the interior. This was our goal. The excitement of visiting a country absolutely devoid of tourists is so rare that one may be pardoned for giving way to it.

Of course one cannot travel here without an escort. Two mounted men accompanied us everywhere in Turkey, and when we again came over the Greek frontier we were met by a sergeant and six privates.

Our first day was nearly all spent in skirting the gulf and plain of Ambrakia. One need not be impatient to get away from that beautiful region. The first object which drew our attention was the ruins of Nikopolis, about an hour out from Prevesa. The city was founded by Augustus as a magnificent trophy of his victory at Actium, at the foot of the hill on which he had pitched his tent before the battle. On sailing into Prevesa the day before, we had passed over the very waters once enlivened by that combat, and over which Antony, forgetting for once to be a soldier, followed the wanton queen in flight and left the world to Augustus.

The ruins of Nikopolis, spread out over several square miles, look imposing in the distance; but, like most Roman ruins near at hand, vulgar in comparison with Greek. The theatre is massive, and the aqueduct inspires respect for the practical sense of the conquerors of the world. The thought that St. Paul spent a winter here gives a peculiar interest to the ruins.

By pressing your way up through a part of the square miles of breast-high thistles about the theatre, you may reach the top of the hill from which Augustus looked down and saw his enemy apparently strong. The whole world for which he was about to grapple affords few scenes of greater beauty than that which lay before his eye.

The road over which our carriage proceeded was a testimonial that the Turks have been misrepresented by the traveller who said:

"It is a favorite idea with all barbarous princes that the badness of the roads adds considerably to the natural strength of their dominions. The Turks and Persians are undoubtedly of this opinion; the public highways are, therefore, neglected, and particularly so toward the frontiers."

The road was being made into a good one, but as long stretches of it were covered with piles of dirt, and on a level three or four feet above the older parts, getting on was attended with difficulty. But the Turks could not be considered devoid of energy when they put so much work upon the road which everybody was then prophesying would in a few years pass into the hands of the Greeks. It may be that the "sick man" thought he might yet use that road for military operations which would trouble his southern neighbors. At any rate he did so.

Along the foot of the mountains which bound the plain of Ambrakia to the north, out from under the well-built road, copious fountains of clear, cold water gush, contributing to the river Luro, the ancient Charadros, which here overflows its banks far and wide; and a most luxuriant tangle of trees and vines, standing often in several inches of water, impenetrable as an Indian jungle, astonishes one accustomed to judge the vegetation of Greece by its eastern parts.

Our second day's journey was up the gorge of the Luro to its sources, and then over a ridge into the plain of Joannina. For six hours we had one continuous vale of Tempe. One does not hear enough of this region. Who, for instance, ever hears of Rogus, a ruin which we passed toward evening on the first day? Yet here is an acropolis which one sees from a great distance— such an imposing affair that I supposed for a long time that it must be Ambrakia. There are remains of fine old Hellenic walls, on which stood Byzantine walls now badly crumbled. Leake supposes Rogus to be the ancient Charadra.

Along with us went a large family of Jews, seeking among the Turks a safer residence than the Ionian Islands, where just then the Jew was made very uncomfortable. As we halted at noon of the first day by a large oak-tree, on the shore of a brook, it was interesting to see groups, Christian, Jew, and Turk, taking their meals at quite an interval from one another, but all under the shade of the same tree. As we came into Joannina, the Jews were subjected to a searching examination, but we were not examined at all. We heard afterward that the father of this family was suspected of bringing a lot of letters, thus defrauding the Turkish Government of its postage fee.

But I have delayed so long over preliminaries that I can hardly be just to Joannina itself. In fact, to be just to Joannina one should write a book, and not an article. As one approaches the great plain and lake surrounded by snow-capped mountains, one feels that here, as now, must always have been the principal settlement of the whole region. The name Joannina (pronounced Yanina) appears in Byzantine annals as early as the ninth century, when mention is made of a bishop of Joannina about three hundred and fifty years after the last mention of a bishop of Dodona. Though not standing on the same site, it is the successor of Dodona. But its history is essentially Turkish. Perhaps its greatest distinction is that it was the capital of Ali Pasha, who, in the first twenty years of the present century, had established, by an energetic unscrupulousness which reminds one of Demosthenes's picture of Philip of Macedon, a sovereignty practically independent of the Sultan, almost as large as the Sultan's other European possessions. Ali had a sort of thirst for blood, which appears not to have belonged to Philip. The Greeks, however, seem to have forgiven him the slaughter of their fathers and mothers in deference to his genius, and to take a local pride in the monster. Most of the stories told about him are records of some murder or other. Most of the compliments which his satellites used to pay him turned on the idea that he was a good butcher. A place in the lake is still pointed out as the scene of the drowning of a dozen or so Greek women whose morals, forsooth, were not up to the high standard which Ali said he was going to set up. Some of them belonged to the best families in Joannina, and could not believe that Ali meant more than blackmail until the waters were closing over them, when they shrieked and grasped at the boat so wildly that the executioners had to become inhuman in order to carry out the commands of their lord.

But this Albanian Mussulman reckoned ill when he threw down the gauntlet to the Sultan. Retiring to an island in the lake, when he could no longer defend his capital, he was first stabbed treacherously in a parley in which he thought he was going to make terms with his master, and finally killed by shots fired through the floor from the room under that in which he had taken refuge. His head and those of his sons, who had not well supported their father in the struggle, were fastened up over the door of the Seraglio in Constantinople.

One afternoon, after conversing awhile with the successor of Ali, the present Vali or Governor-General of Epirus, if it can be called conversing to take a cup of coffee with a man, and see him smoke a cigarette, giving you meanwhile a few of his thoughts through an interpreter, we went over to the island, and saw the room in a monastery where Ali was slain. The floor was well perforated with bullet-holes.

Ali had unwittingly paved the way for Greek independence. He had shown that the power of the Sultan might be resisted for a while at least. Some of the leaders of the Greeks, who made his camp their school of war, felt that the evoking of a grand national sentiment would make them able to resist to the end. When Ali fell in 1822, Greece was already in arms.

Joannina, in the days of Ali, had, if we may believe reports, a population of 50,000. It has now not more than half that number. The Greeks are about three-quarters of the whole population, the other quarter being divided between Turks and Jews, with considerable preponderance in favor of the former, who still hold all the offices, and show by their bearing that they are the ruling class. One evening we visited the castle, which occupies a peninsula jutting out into the lake, made an island by a moat across the neck. It was positively scandalous the way those soldiers went in rags. Even the noncommissioned officers, with their torn chevrons, seemed in harmony with the walls and barracks, now tumbling to decay. But these awkward, ragged fellows seemed to have signs of strength about them, and might give a good report of themselves in battle. We lingered long over one big gun, which bore marks of service at Shipka Pass. We were reminded then that it would not do to leave out the Turk entirely in the settlement of the Eastern question.

To the west of Joannina the population is largely Albanian. This class of Albanians makes you feel that there may be some truth in the words of an English traveller, who, in classifying the Albanians, speaks of one class as "Albanians who never change their clothes." The chronology of some of these garments of more than a hundred heterogeneous pieces would be an interesting study. Rags are generally picturesque, and these Albanians contribute somewhat to the picturesqueness of Joannina's streets. They wear for the most part a white fez, darkened by age and dirt, which distinguishes them from the people of the city, who wear, almost to a man, the red fez. On one or two occasions when Mr. Hill started to take a photograph in the streets, before he could set up his camera, a perfect sea of red heads was formed in front of it, and the very zeal to be photographed frustrated the attempt. It was almost like evoking a mob.

But in Joannina, of all places in the world, one must not forget the past, the great Hellenic past. This region was once called Hellopia and the inhabitants

Selloi, a variation for Helloi, and from here the name appears to have been transmitted to the whole of Hellas. It is quite a testimonial to the persistency of the old Hellenic spirit that travellers all notice how pure is the Greek spoken in Joannina.

Three hours' ride across a range of hills to the south lies Dodona, at the foot of Mount Tomarus, which at the time of our visit (in May) was heavily capped with snow. This oldest oracle and sanctuary of Greece, famous before Delphi was born, has a situation only a little less imposing than Delphi. Until about twenty-five years ago one was still in doubt in just what part of this region to look for the old famous sanctuary. But at that time Carapanos, a wealthy Greek, settled that question with the spade.

Procuring from the library, by the kindness of the professor of French in the Lyceum, the two beautiful volumes in which Carapanos has given the results of his work, I took them with me to the spot where he found Dodona, and followed in his footsteps. This library, by the way, contains a good many valuable books, new and old, but they are huddled together in very close quarters, as the librarian sadly admitted, employing the English phrase "pell-mell." But worse than the disorder was the dampness. Carapanos's book of plates was mildewed and fallen apart. Rich Greeks probably think their benefactions more safely bestowed in Athens. Otherwise somebody would have given a new library building to Joannina.

The walls that Carapanos discovered all have a singularly late appearance, and there is a striking lack of pottery in the ground; but the inscriptions and dedicatory offerings leave no doubt that this is Dodona. The temples and the finely built theatre, one of the largest in Greece, doubtless supplied the place of older and ruder buildings of the time when all Hellas came to hear the voice of Father Zeus in the rustling oak-leaves.

At the southeastern end of the lake of Joannina is a hill called Kastritza, crowned by fortifications indicating the existence of just such a city as one would look for to match this great plain and lake. Here are walls about three miles in circuit, and, in a considerable part of their extent, twenty feet high and twelve feet thick, of the finest polygonal work. And yet, so little is known of the history of Epirus, that even the name of this city cannot be ascertained with certainty. Leake thought it was Dodona itself, placing the sanctuary, however, at a little distance, on the spot now occupied by Joannina. Kastritza might still be regarded as a possible candidate for Dodona, inasmuch as sanctuaries in Greece were often at quite a remove from the nearest town, as in the case of Epidauros and Oropos. But the fact that very little is known of any *city* called Dodona, as well as the fact on the other side that the sanctuary excavated by Carapanos has a small acropolis connected with it, makes it extremely improbable that this great city, Kastritza, was Dodona.

The picturesqueness of the city of Joannina is matched by its grand setting. Its lake is over a thousand feet above the sea, and streams from the amphitheatre of the snow-covered mountains keep flowing into it without finding any visible outlet. The color upon the mountains and the lake at sunrise and sunset is often wonderful. Mount Mitzikeli, which rises abruptly from the lake on its side opposite the city, is a breeder of thunder-storms. (It must be remembered that this was the abode of Jupiter Tonans in antiquity.) Sometimes at mid-day, when the sun is shining to the east and west of Joannina, a storm-cloud will come down over this mountain from the higher ones of the Pindus range back of it and make straight for the city. What a place for a painter! Leake tells of the difficulty he had in persuading the Italian painter, Lusieri, to stay beyond a day or two here because he thought he detected symptoms of malaria; but, adds Leake:

"The picturesque beauties of the place had such a powerful attraction for him that he was induced to hazard a longer visit, until his fears having been calmed by my own experience, and that of the Joanninites in general, he prolonged his stay for six weeks. The longer he remained the more he was impressed with the feeling that in the great sources of his art, the sublime and beautiful, and in their exquisite mixture and contrast, Joannina exceeds every place he had seen in Italy or Greece."

It is a pity that the pictures which Lusieri painted here were lost at sea.

The exit from this place, where tourists are never seen and where newspapers are strictly prohibited, into the Greek world of talk and bustle was as interesting as the approach to it. Our road lay over the great pass of the Pindos into Thessaly, the pass over which Julius Cæsar led his army, when he was about to grapple with Pompey. For the first day's ride the Arachthos was our road. We crossed it more than twenty times, when it was a credit to our horses not to be carried down the stream. Of course, keeping one's feet entirely out of the water was impossible. At last we came to the end of that day's journey, where the stream had dwindled to a harmless looking brook at the Wallachian town of Metzovo. These Wallachians, especially the women, look entirely different from the people round about. They talk a sort of Latin and are supposed to be a remnant of the old Roman colony of Dacia. The quaint old town, where this curious old people is wedged in among other peoples, is within two hours of the backbone of Pindos, over which we passed the next morning. Within an area of a few square miles here nearly all the rivers of Greece that flow all the year round have their head waters.

It was with something of a feeling of exaltation that we left our Turkish guards behind at the ridge of Pindos and soon found ourselves tracing the ever-widening streamlet, which was soon to become the broad Peneios, down into the land of the Greeks, not only of Greek gods and heroes of the past, but of the Greek men of to-day, who have at last here inherited what their fathers possessed.

THE BICYCLE IN GREECE

It has been repeatedly suggested to me, by the regrets of a considerable number of the members of the American School at Athens, that I should give some public expression to the utility of the bicycle in Greece. I put aside certain temptations to praise the bicycle generally, and speak of it only as a help here in the study of archæology.

Every year men come to us saying: "I left my wheel at home, thinking it would be of little use in this rough country." After some reflection on the difficulty of having it sent over after them, they rent wheels a few times, after which, deterred partly by the awkwardness of having to hunt up a wheel for every little excursion, and partly by suffering from the poorer quality of wheels that are to be had on loan, they drop the habit of bicycling. But the wheel has been so keenly appreciated here by generations of students that this dropping out is to be very much deprecated. Archæology does not consist entirely in the study of books and museums. That it does largely so consist it must be confessed; but a legitimate and important part of Greek archæology is the knowledge of the face of the country; the tracing out of its ancient routes, going over the passes and climbing now and then a mountain; the skirting its coasts; the visiting its places of great renown; the studying of its battle-fields; and the seeing of the landscapes on which rested the eyes of Pericles and Epaminondas, of Sophocles and Pindar. Especially important is this for one who has but one year to spend in Greece. It is well for him, even at the expense of some time which might well be spent in the museum or in the library, so to fill his mind with the landscapes of Greece that, when he goes back and stands before his classes and speaks, for example, of Leuctra, he may be looking with the mind's eye upon the slopes down which the Spartans came charging, the opposite slope where the Thebans stood, and the valley between, where they clashed. The class is then sure to catch some of this vivid presentation, and feel that they have almost seen Leuctra themselves. If, then, one should spend the whole of his year in museums and libraries, we might say to him, "This ought ye to have done, and not to have left the other undone."

Granted that one wishes to see the country and to become familiar with it, so that he will read Greek history, and Greek poetry, too, with other eyes, the bicycle becomes evidently indispensable. To take an example: One morning, to shake off a headache incurred by sitting too long in a close room at an invaluable meeting of the German School the night before, I bicycled with a member of our school, who had never been there before, to Liopesi (Pæania), the birthplace of Demosthenes, stayed long enough to chat with the villagers and take a glass of their resined wine, with which one is supposed to drink in the gift of talking modern Greek, and came back to Athens, all in three hours, taking it very leisurely at that, and returning by a roundabout way, reached home full of oxygen and *sans* headache. We might have walked, to be sure, but not to Pæania, unless we had given the whole day to it.

Railroads will take you already to many parts of Greece, and one can now proceed by rail from the northern border of Thessaly to Kalamata at the southern end of Messenia. But even railroads cannot do all for us that the bicycle does. Exercise, open air, and, perhaps more than all, the delight in propelling one's self, will make one prefer the wheel. We can reach Eleusis by bicycle as quickly as the train takes us, and choose our own time for starting, without the alternative of sitting some time at the station or losing the train.

There are many other charming spots in Attica where no railroad comes in to help. Marathon and Salamis are two such places, to which we make excursions every year. One afternoon in May two of us started out from Athens at half-past two, proceeding aimlessly eastward against a rather pronounced wind. Suddenly the thought struck us that Marathon lay in front of us. A definite goal is always inspiring, and we struck a good gait for Marathon. We reached it before five o'clock, and after passing ten minutes on the top of the historic mound came back to Athens for dinner at quarter before eight. Last year some of us rode out on Thanksgiving Day through Dekeleia to a point where we saw Oropos and the Eubœan Gulf at our feet, and Dirphys, the highest mountain in Eubœa, rising opposite us, and then turned around with the recollection of one of the finest views in the world to add to enjoyment of our Thanksgiving dinner. In twenty minutes, had we so wished, we could have been in Oropos. On any day, one can start out from Athens and reach the end of Attica in any direction, and get home to an early dinner. In fact, we have sometimes taken dinner at home after straying as far as Megara and Thebes. The acquaintance which some members of our school have gained with Attica, in all its nooks and corners, by single day's bicycle-riding, is something noteworthy; and when, in 1897, on Thanksgiving Day, we turned out ten men for a ride across Salamis to Megara for a luncheon, and came home by the shore road, we felt considerable *esprit de corps.*

The notion of foreigners that the roads of Greece are bad compared with those of other countries is an error. A bicycle journey through Italy and Sicily disabused me of that notion. The worst road that I ever tried was that between Caserta and Naples, and the next worse was that leading into Rome from the north. There are, of course, some bad roads in Greece; but even Sicily, to say nothing of worse roads in Italy, cured me of complaining against Greece. For a pure pleasure ride, the road between Tripolitza and Sparta would be hard to match anywhere in the world. It is in capital condition, and, on account of its gentle grade, involves very little walking. Six hours suffice for the journey in either direction, and the view either way is superb. The ride through Ætolia and Acarnania, regions considered half civilized in the classical period of Greek history, but always fine in natural beauty, with big lakes, and rivers that "move in majesty" (a rare thing in Greece), and hedged in by high mountains, is perhaps the best in Greece. One rides from the shore of the Corinthian Gulf opposite Patras to Arta (Ambrakia) in two days, with a comfortable night at Agrinion, passing the historic Messolonghi and visiting the ruins of Calydon, Pleuron, Œniadæ, Stratos, Limnæa, and Amphilochian Argos, while to the right and left are other ruins which invite one to make détours if one is not in a hurry. And one ought not to omit the recently excavated Thermon, the ancient capital of Ætolia, even if it does cost an extra day. The long-known and impressive ruins of Œniadæ, the chief city in Acarnania, also invite one to linger a whole day instead of spending a few hours in passing.

The first five cities of ancient Greece in renown and interest were Athens, Sparta, Argos, Thebes, and Corinth. One can ride from Athens to Thebes or Corinth and back in a single day; he can also reach Argos from Athens in a day, leaving a rather long day's work for reaching Sparta. Any good bicyclist would find it no great matter to leave Thebes and pay his respects to Athens on the first day, visit Corinth and Argos on the next day, and sleep comfortably at Sparta the next night.

One day in February the clouds dissipated themselves in such a way as to make me believe that we were about to have a few days of that winter weather which is "rarer than a day in June," and so, taking a train to Eleusis, to spare myself a little at the start, I rode over the famous Treis Kephalai Pass into Bœotia. I thought when I was at the top of the pass that the view presented was the finest in Greece. Not to mention lesser glories, Parnassus was close at hand on the left, Dirphys almost equally close on the right, while very distant, but very clear, directly in front, was "snowy Olympus," a perfect mass of white. After lunching at Thebes, I wheeled easily along to Lebadea, entering it as the setting sun was turning the white mountains into pink. The next day, more clear and beautiful than the first, if that were possible, brought me to Lamia in Thessaly, via Chæronea, Doris, and Thermopylæ. The third day, in order to get a nearer view of Olympus, I rode and climbed up to the top of the ridge which formed the old border between Greece and Turkey, before Thessaly was incorporated into the kingdom of Greece, and on which, in the late war, the Greeks made their last stand after the battle of Domoko. From this point Olympus is, indeed, grander than from the passes of Cithæron, while the whole Pindos range, and the grand isolated peak of Tymphrestos, which some think would prove, if properly measured, to be the highest peak in Greece, stand up in majesty. Parnassus and the Ætolian Mountains make a fine showing on the south. From this point, on this same third day, as clear as the two preceding, I reached Amphissa at evening, after climbing two passes and enjoying new glories at each. It was, in fact, a continuous intoxication, to recover from which it required two days of archæological study at Delphi. This was, to be sure, almost equally intoxicating, but, being an intoxication of another sort, it let me down gently. In three days I had got a glimpse of nearly all Greece in such weather as only a Greek winter can give.

ACARNANIA

In many respects the most interesting journey which I have made in Greece was my last one through Acarnania and Ætolia. To be sure, my last journey in Greece is always my best one; yet there was a special attraction in this journey from the fact that it was the fulfilment of a long-cherished desire. There was a gap in my knowledge of western Greece which I keenly felt. I had tramped over the Ionian Islands, visited Joannina and Dodona, and passed over the Pindos range into Thessaly. In passing Prevesa and Nikopolis the sight of the Ambrakian Gulf had filled me with a desire to explore its innermost recesses. The grand mountains of Acarnania to the south challenged especially to a nearer view. Three years later, coming up from Patras by the Northwestern Railroad of Greece to Agrinion, the capital of Ætolia, I had visited in bad weather Œniadæ, the most important city of Acarnania, mused over the Ætolian acropolis of Calydon, famous in song and story, and gone as far north as Stratos, Acarnania's capital; but although in looking out from Stratos it seems as if all the glory was farther north, my travelling companion was obliged to retreat, and I followed his fortunes. All this had but whetted my appetite; and, three years later, at the end of February in that most marvellous of winters, which gave us six consecutive weeks of April temperature with unclouded sky, I set out from Piræus one moonlight night to satisfy my desire, with a companion who was not in a hurry.

Our first goal was Arta, the terminus of a line of steamers from Piræus. No mean part of the journey on a clear winter day is the view of the three masses of snow-covered mountains to the north of the Corinthian Gulf, each over eight thousand feet high, and the three to the south, falling just short of the same height, to say nothing of many others which would be impressive if the giants were absent. The effect is not unlike that of Lake Lucerne somewhat broadened out. A stop at Samos, in Kephallenia, on the morning of the second day, and a sail between Kephallenia and Ithaca, during which the latter may be studied at short range, is no slight advantage "thrown in." At Leukas, in the afternoon, came a stirring scene. About a hundred recruits were taken on board. Greece had had troops in Crete for a week, and so, although war had not actually been declared, she was gathering troops to protect her border or to advance into Epirus, as circumstances might dictate. Two hours later, in sailing through the waters where the battle of Actium took place, we passed under the guns of the Turkish forts at Prevesa. As the Greek color-bearer was inclined to flaunt his flag a good deal, it seemed something like an adventure. But the Margarita escaped the fate that a few weeks later overtook the Macedonia, which was sunk by the Turkish fire, while the passengers had to swim for their lives. At Vonitza we took on another hundred of the recruits pouring into Arta from all over western Greece. The men were cheerful and orderly, but brimful of the war feeling which pervaded Greece.

Delayed by these embarkations of troops, we did not reach Koprena, the port of Arta, until eight o'clock in the evening. Then there was a lack of boats to bring such a crowd to shore, and with a long drive of ten or twelve miles in the dark, over a bad road crowded with soldiers, it was after midnight when we reached Arta. Our host, a man whom I had never seen, but to whom I was introduced by a friend in Athens, had been waiting for us at Koprena since noon, and did not appear to think that he had done any more for us than any proper man would do.

TEMPLE AT STRATOS.

The next morning, with a captain of artillery who had been our fellow-passenger from Athens, we went out through orange groves to the famous bridge of Arta, over the Arachthos, which here forms the border, the Greeks having secured, in 1881, Arta and its adjacent fields up to the river, along with Thessaly. The present border is the most unrighteous one that could be devised. A river is generally no proper boundary-line, but in this case especially it is intolerable. The plain across the river belongs by nature to the city, and, in fact, is owned largely by the people of Arta, who have suffered manifold inconveniences in the management of their property. Who can wonder that the Greeks were anxious for an offensive campaign here which should give them back their own?

The finest feature of Arta is its view. From the hill, at the foot of which lies the city, one sees the mountains near Dodona, and farther south and quite close at hand, is Tsoumerka, in the spring a mass of snow, falling just short of eight thousand feet. Behind this, over beyond the Acheloos, the snowy peaks of the Pindos range crowd one upon another in such thick array that one despairs of identifying them all with the names given on the map. To the south lie the three mountains of Acarnania in *echelon*, impressive although only a little over five thousand feet high, and the glorious gulf itself.

Arta has also a history. One hurries by the interesting Church of the Consoling Virgin, a brick structure of the tenth century, perhaps, and a mediæval castle, to the days when Arta was Ambrakia. Even the days when it was the capital of the famous Pyrrhus seem recent, compared with the really great days when it was a democratic city of free Hellas long before the Persian war. Cropping out from under the shabby houses of the town are walls made of massive blocks which speak of days of greatness. This blooming colony of Corinth, foreordained by its situation to be the principal city of the region, gave its name in antiquity, as now, to the great gulf which it overlooks.

Corinth had the misfortune, rare in Greek history, to plant one unfilial colony, Corcyra, which, as early as 665 B.C., worsted the mother in a great naval battle, and, from a daughter, became a lasting enemy. To recover her influence in these regions, Corinth, in the days of Kypselos and Periander, which seem pretty old days, planted Ambrakia besides Anaktorion, just inside the entrance of the gulf, and Leukas just outside. As if to prove that Corinth was not an especially hard mother, these colonies always remained filial, and their contingents were always drawn up in the Persian war alongside those of Corinth. Ambrakia, besides dominating the rich plain which by nature belongs to her, but by the will of Europe now belongs to Turkey, had also an especial significance as standing on the road to Dodona for nearly all of Greece.

But it is not my purpose to rewrite any portion of the history of Greece, but only to set forth clearly the physical and moral position of Ambrakia, that one may realize more clearly the satisfaction of the sturdy Demosthenes, the man of deeds, not the man of words, when, at Olpæ and under the walls of Amphilochian Argos, a few miles to the south, he crippled Ambrakia as thoroughly as Cleomenes had crippled Argos at Tiryns a few years before the Persian war, and made Corinth feel in the woes of her favorite daughter that she had not kindled the flames of the Peloponnesian war with impunity. Since certain Messenians took part in this battle, it has been supposed by some that the famous Nike of Pæonios at Olympia was set up to commemorate their share of the victory.

We proceeded southward from Arta by a very good carriage-road skirting the west end of the gulf. About one-third of our day's journey was taken up in traversing the famous Makrynoros Pass, where the mountains, as high as Hymettus, come down almost perpendicularly to the sea for a space of about ten miles. This is called the Thermopylæ of western Greece; but it is a much more difficult pass to force than Thermopylæ, where two foot-hills come down to the sea with a more gentle slope. Thermopylæ, too, in modern times has lost its original character by the formation of quite a plain at the foot of its mountains by the alluvial deposit of the Spercheios and the incrustation formed by sulphur springs; while Makrynoros remains a mountain running straight down into the sea, necessitating the making of the modern carriage-road with great difficulty and expense. But as this road is a thousand feet above the water, it affords a fine view over the gulf and its setting. The railroad which connects Patras with Agrinion must come some day to Arta, so all the people of the region were saying. The Makrynoros Pass would be the chief difficulty in the way; but the railroad could keep the same height all the way, and no steep grades would be required. The main difficulty would be the crossing of the many gullies which run down from the side of the mountain. In the ordinary march of events, Arta will be included in the slowly extending network, although the claims of Sparta may have to be attended to first. It depends somewhat upon the relative influence and push of the delegates of the sections concerned.

This pass has a strategic importance, and we may soon hear of it again in connection with military operations. The Ambrakian Gulf and Maliac Gulf, by Thermopylæ, reach out toward each other, making what is sometimes called an isthmus, an echo of the Isthmus of Corinth; but if anyone tries to make his way across this he will realize that it is only an isthmus by courtesy, and will have vividly impressed upon his mind that "the longest way around is the shortest way home." The pass of Thermopylæ may be circumvented; but so piled up are the mountains to the west of Makrynoros that, in order to circumvent it, one might as well go to Thermopylæ itself.

In the Greek war of independence, the first severe defeat of the Greeks took place in the second year of the war, near the northern end of Makrynoros. Maurocordatos, the President of the new State, wishing to be a Washington and to be general as well as statesman, took command of the regular army, and pushed northward through the pass, as if to take the offensive against the Turks at Arta, and then, as if not quite certain what he wanted to do, waited for the Turks to attack him, which they did in good time, annihilating his army at Peta. His head-quarters were farther back at the opening of the pass. Had he decided to take the defensive soon enough he might have immortalized Makrynoros and saved his army, instead of simply saving himself and his staff. At Peta, which lay on the hill to the left of our road from Arta to the mouth of the pass, is a tablet on which are inscribed the names of the members of the regiment of Philhellenes who, to give the Greeks an example, stood their ground until they were all shot down, except twenty-five, who succeeded in cutting their way through the enemy.

In the battle fought near the south end of the pass in which Demosthenes crushed the Ambrakians, the pass played no rôle at all. Here our road passed between Olpæ and Amphilochian Argos, and half an hour was well spent in making a part of the circuit of the walls of the latter, which are fairly well preserved. A sure token that Amphilochian Argos lay here, and not at Karvasara, as was once supposed, is the name of the plain between the old walls and the sea. This still bears the name "Vlichia," which is all that is left of "Amphilochia"; but it is enough to prove the identity.

At evening we came to Karvasara, at the foot of one of the most imposing acropolises in Greece. Here we were in Acarnania, where, as in Ætolia, it is more difficult to find names for imposing remains than to find remains for important names. But it is quite likely that the name Limnæa will stick to this great acropolis, inasmuch as Limnæa lay on the sea, and its name is justified by the presence of something half lake and half marsh that almost laps its walls on the south, or landward, side, although certain distances given in Polybius do not quite tally with this identification. From this elevation we could look to the south farther than Stratos, which was hidden by a bend of the long mountain at the south end of which it lay. I had in a certain sense joined hands with my former journey, although the best of the present journey, which was cumulative in its enjoyment, was still to come.

Among many walled cities of Acarnania the three most important are Limnæa, Stratos, and Œniadæ. Limnæa, which plays a comparatively insignificant rôle in history, has the most commanding position, on a high hill overlooking the east end of the Ambrakian Gulf. The walls are well preserved, and, for their height as well as extent, excite admiration. Stratos, situated on the west bank of the Acheloos, is not quite so high, but its walls are fully as extensive and high. It has also well-preserved foundations of a temple of white limestone. It confronted Agrinion, the capital city of the Ætolians, the eternal enemies of the Acarnanians; and these two grim fortress capitals frowned at each other for ages with nothing but the rolling river between them.

But Œniadæ is, after all, the most impressive of all the Acarnanian ruins. It crowns an irregular hill which was once an island, but has become a part of the mainland by the action of the Acheloos. Down to the fourth century before Christ, and perhaps even later, the sea touched its western side, for here are clear traces of a harbor, as well as some fairly preserved ship-sheds. The walls are not only of great extent, but wonderfully well preserved, with gates of most varied forms, in which the arch is seen in various stages of formation. The whole vast enclosure is covered with a grove of great oaks, which, in some cases, have pushed down the walls. In one case, the growing oak has pulled out one stone from its place and carried it up in its embrace several feet above the rest of the wall. So luxuriant is the vegetation all over the hill that one who will see the whole wall outside and inside—and no less will satisfy one—must give up a whole day to the task, and force his way through thorns and briers that scratch and tear, paying with his person.

The result of four or five visits to Œniadæ was finally a plan to make excavations there, and, in 1901, several members of the American School undertook the work. With a comparatively small outlay of money, but with great hardship, they laid bare a theatre, mostly rock-cut, with many inscriptions, the ship-sheds, and near by them a bath. The theatre is most picturesque. Anyone who fails to visit Œniadæ makes a mistake.

ÆTOLIA

On my first visit to Ætolia and Acarnania I went in at the front door, *i.e.*, by the Northwestern Railroad from Patras, past Calydon, renowned in legend, and Messolonghi, of deathless fame, to Agrinion, the terminus of the railroad, and thence northward. On the second visit I went in at the back door by steamer to Arta, and journeyed southward. On a third visit I jumped in, as it were, at the window.

Having returned from a flying visit to Olympia, I and my companion met at Patras two other members of the American School, with whom we intended to bicycle as far north as Arta, diverging to the right and left to visit a half-dozen ancient sites of the region. But twenty-four hours of heavy rain made us feel that the Messolonghi route would be nothing but a bed of mud; and we let the morning boat of the Northwestern Railroad cross over in the rain without us. When at eleven o'clock it was clear, I proposed that we should take a sail-boat over to Naupaktos, and push our way up into Ætolia from that point. Since a good part of the way would be uphill, the water would have run off and the road would be passable. I should at least get something new out of the journey, and realize how short was the distance which separated the Lake of Agrinion (Trichonis) from the Corinthian Gulf. We could see by the map that this was not more than twelve miles as the crow flies, and I pictured to myself some water-shed from which we should see both the sea and the lake.

We sailed to the point called now Kastro Roumelias, the ancient Antirrhion, and mounted our wheels at half-past one. Three-quarters of an hour brought us to Naupaktos. This city was flourishing in the seventh and sixth centuries before Christ; but its plain was not large enough, and the places in the interior to which it was a key were not important enough to give it permanent prosperity. In the fifth century it was taken by the Athenians, and given to the exiled Messenians, who made it a stanch ally of Athens in the sphere of Corinthian influence. Besides being most picturesquely situated, it has looked down on important events. Under its walls and in its harbor Phormio, the Athenian admiral, twice annihilated a Peloponnesian fleet of more than double the size of his own. The greatest naval battle that ever took place between Christendom and Islam, though fought in the open sea twenty miles to the west, was named after it, because the Turkish armada set out from it to meet Don John of Austria. One hardly recognizes the name in the Venetian form, Lepanto. The Greek name of to-day, Epaktos, is nearer to the ancient form.

We stopped only a few minutes here, as our intention was to reach Kephalovrysi (Thermon) that night, and, if we failed in that, it seemed child's-play to reach at least Makrinou on the lake. Even when bicycling ceased and we settled down to steady climbing, we felt no misgivings; and when at four o'clock we began to descend we thought our work for the day about finished. But our confidence was rudely shaken when we saw before us the broad, pebbly bed of the Evenos, which flows down through these mountains, taking a sharp turn to the west and passing under the walls of Calydon. We had forgotten to reckon with this. We now paid dearly for our descent by another climb, which seemed unending, and before we reached our greatest altitude far from Kephalovrysi, and, for aught we knew, far from Makrinou also, it became dark.

This road seems an excellent example of the way in which the little kingdom of Greece ought not to make internal improvements. The fine carriage-road, built at great expense, winds with gentlest grade along every projection and indentation of the mountains; and yet we met on our whole journey to the top only a single cart, and in many places the road was so overgrown with grass that no ruts appeared. When it was growing dark we saw another reason why the road might not be popular. In some places it had slipped downhill; and in other places the hills had slipped down into it, which was almost as bad. There is no call for a fine highway from Naupaktos to the lake. The great interior basin of Ætolia is provided with a good course for its traffic *via* Messolonghi; and no power on earth can force it to come this way. It is useless for some silly people in Naupaktos to complain that favoritism was shown in not laying out the Northwestern Railroad with their town as a starting-point. For a town doomed to decline, a steamer stopping two or three times a week, supplemented by sail-boats to and from the more lively and more important southern shore of the Corinthian Gulf, may well suffice. The Northwestern Railroad will soon be prolonged to Arta, giving to him that hath, according to the habit of railroads; and even this finely built carriage-road will continue to be avoided by every self-respecting traveller, as it is now, until only pieces of this monumental folly shall remain. The demarch of Kephalovrysi told me that the primary object of this road was to enable the Government to move troops by land in case of the blockade of the coast by stronger Powers. But even with that explanation the road seems useless without good roads farther east to connect with it, to say nothing of the futility of Greece attempting to resist the stronger naval Powers.

When darkness was fairly upon us, and just as we were beginning to descend, we found a wretched village of four or five houses. At one of these with a wine-shop below and living-rooms above, we were well fed, but in a rather primitive style, I eating my rice from the same bowl with the host, as we all sat cross-legged in front of the fire. Since it was very cold, we were glad to lie down for the night on rugs, with other rugs over us, with our feet to the fire, making one end of a semicircle, at the other end of which was the host with his wife and five small children, while below, in the business part of the establishment, were five larger children.

When we got off at sunrise the next morning, the view to the west was something over which one may well grow enthusiastic. Low down at our feet, but stretching far away to the west, was the lake which we had sought, and beyond its farther end another smaller one. At that farther end, too, was the fertile plain of Agrinion, where grows the best tobacco in Greece. Beyond that and across the Acheloos rose the snowy mountains of Acarnania and Leukas, just touched by the rising sun. On our right, rising up from the north shore of the lake and stretching far to the north, were the gigantic mountains which make the larger and wilder part of Ætolia. On our left were the lower peaks of Mount Arakynthos bordering the lake on the south. This is the heart of Ætolia. It has a wonderfully drawing power to one who has once seen it. The lake, enclosed by mountains on its eastern end, and on its western end by a plain, is wonderfully beautiful. It is striking that its surface is hardly stirred by either row-boats or sail-boats. The only time I ever saw a sail upon it was on this particular morning.

It was matter for sad reflection that this great plain did not all belong to Ætolia, but that the part beyond the Acheloos was Acarnania. Rivers cannot divide peoples; and these two peoples through all their history dyed this unnatural boundary with their blood. The Ætolians, as the stronger if not the better people, generally succeeded in keeping a foothold on the other bank, holding even Stratos, the capital of Acarnania, and Œniadæ, its strongest city, for periods of centuries. But the Acarnanians were tough antagonists, and never said die till all was merged in the supremacy of Rome.

It was a matter of a few minutes to spin down to Makrinou, which now had for us no importance. Kephalovrysi was our goal. The visit was for me tinged with some melancholy reflections. Less than a year before I had been there with my friend, Charles Peabody, of Cambridge, and we had been much excited at the thought that here lay Thermon, the head of the Ætolian League, and so near the surface that a little excavation would prove it. On my return to Athens I asked the Ephor General of Antiquities to reserve the spot for us, which he said he would do. But a few months later, when the Greek Archæological Society sent Georgios Soteiriades into Ætolia to explore sites, this one was not excepted; and he attacked it with great success. While I had to rejoice that archæology had gained a triumph, I was sorry that an enthusiastic American had not been the instrument. After a few miles of level road along the east end of the lake, we toiled four or five miles up along the face of the mountain enclosing it on the north side, and then turning sharply away from the lake at Petrochori, a village perched on the top of a ridge commanding as good a view as the one already described, in a few minutes we had reached our goal.

Kephalovrysi has about a thousand inhabitants. It was not more than ten minutes after we had settled ourselves in an eating-house when all the boys of the place and most of the men, with a small representation of the girls, gathered around and thronged in at the door, in spite of the kicks and cuffs of the proprietor. Before we had fairly begun to eat, the demarch appeared with his inseparable companion, the young schoolmaster, the two who had last year escorted us to the ruins, at the head of the whole school, which had been given a half-holiday in honor of our arrival. This time it was a holiday without special dispensation; but the boys were so absorbed in our bicycles, which were the first ever seen in the place, that we had the demarch and the schoolmaster almost to ourselves on the walk out to the ruins.

The excavation of these ruins called Palæo-Bazaar closes a chapter in the topographical study of Ætolia, which began with Colonel Leake. Pouqueville, indeed, prompted by the natural desire to give names to the impressive ruins that met him on every hand, gave names, as he himself confessed, "by a sort of lucky inspiration." A passage in Polybius forms the basis for the topography of this central region of Ætolia. It is the passage in which he describes how Philip V., the young King of Macedon, in 218 B.C., by a forced march from the Acheloos, near Stratos, reached and destroyed Thermon in revenge for the destruction of Dodona in the preceding year by the Ætolians, under Dorymachos. In this narrative he mentions several towns to the right and left of the line of march.

THERMON. TEMPLE OF APOLLO IN THE FOREGROUND

Leake, who never travelled around the east end of the lake, made up his mind that Thermon must be found at Vlocho, the most impressive ruin and strongest fortified place in Ætolia, not far east of Agrinion. Starting with this as a fact, he laid out the rest of the topography accordingly. Two great difficulties, however, confronted Leake. Polybius speaks of the lake as covering the left of the army during a considerable part of the march, while Leake, placing Thermon at Vlocho, cannot keep them from leaving it well to their right all the way. The great topographer, who had successfully located Calydon by transposing two passages in Strabo and inserting a negative, thought it not venturesome to "restore" right for left in this passage of Polybius, on the ground that there are many occurrences of such slips in ancient writers. A second difficulty troubled him less. A march from the Acheloos to Thermon, which is spoken of as a forced march, a record march if you will, from the dawn of a summer day till late in the afternoon, by hardy troops, cannot, if Vlocho is Thermon, be spun out to more than fifteen miles, and that mostly over good ground. Leake talks loosely of arrival at two o'clock in the afternoon, which hardly does justice to the πολλῆς ὥρας of the text.

The prestige of Leake, his almost established record of never going astray, led topographers generally to follow him, at least in the location of Thermon. Bazin, indeed, having a conscience about changing left to right, makes Philip march clear round the lake and reach Vlocho in season to destroy that great citadel on the same day, a distance of forty-five miles over some very bad ground, and that, too, on top of a forced march the day before. A military man like Leake could not have made this error, though he led Bazin into it by falsely locating Thermon.

In spite of a growing belief, starting with Bursian and at last finding exact expression in Lolling's selection of Palæo-Bazaar, that Thermon was somewhere near the east end of the lake, Vlocho, the mighty hill fortress, made such an impression that many regarded the discussion as one in which it was still worth while to sum up the *pros* and *cons*, adding: "If Vlocho is not Thermon, give us some adequate name for it." But the spade, which has again substantiated its claims to be the best archæologist, has relegated all this discussion to the limbo of old notions. Whatever Vlocho was, it was *not* Thermon. A score or more of inscriptions found by Soteiriades at Palæo-Bazaar, speaking of the affairs of the Ætolian League, show that he has found the capital. What makes the identification absolutely certain is the inscription containing the treaty between the Ætolians and Philip of Macedon, in which it is provided that of two copies one shall be set up at Thermon, and the other at Delphi, which was at the time the ecclesiastical capital of the league. The French have found one copy at Delphi; Soteiriades found the other, an exact duplicate, at Kephalovrysi. After that, one surely need not go elsewhere to seek for Thermon. A suggestive trifle was found here before the excavations, viz., a life-size bronze thumb of good work, showing the dint of a hammer on the knuckle. This probably belonged to one of the two thousand statues destroyed by Philip.

Leaving Kephalovrysi at two o'clock, instead of taking the shortest road to Agrinion along the north shore of the lake, at my suggestion, which again sprung from the desire of seeing something new, we circled the lake, following the line of Philip's retreat along the south side, and identifying among other places the site of Trichonion, which gave its name to the lake. Passing between this lake and its neighbor to the west, we reached Agrinion just before dark, and found there a new, clean hotel. The railroad is beginning to work its wonders even in Agrinion.

This flourishing town of about ten thousand inhabitants, the centre of the most important tobacco-growing region in Greece, and the capital of Ætolia, has stolen its name from ancient Agrinion, which lay about seven miles away on the Acheloos. Its real name is Vrachori, which is still used by many who do not fancy the revamping of classical names, especially when they are foisted on to towns that are not entitled to them, and have an honorable history of their own which has been gained under the name which it is proposed to set aside. Vrachori is such a case.

Not till after dinner did we present ourselves at the house of the doctor who had bountifully entertained my friend and me last year for two nights. Both he and his wife seemed hurt that we had not all four of us come unannounced straight to them, and extorted from us the promise that on our return from Arta we would spend a night with them. "But these things lay on the knees of the gods." After starting off hopefully in the morning, when almost in sight of Stratos my bicycle met with a collapse, which we tried in vain to remedy; and the afternoon train bore me in great tribulation through the front door of Ætolia back to Patras and Athens.

The next year, and pretty nearly every succeeding year, brought me again to this most romantic part of Greece, so little known by modern travellers, and so little famed in ancient history, but full of walls and acropolises which cry out for a name. On the last of these visits we climbed Vlocho on a rather hot day. To judge from the exhaustion which even the strongest felt, as well as from the appearance of the mountain, for Vlocho is really a mountain, we have here the highest acropolis in Greece. It looks down upon Trichonis to the south and back into the rugged peaks of Ætolia to the north, overtopping all the foot-hills of those mountains. Its walls also match the commanding position. It is no wonder that Leake took it for the great central citadel of the Ætolians, none other than Thermon. But not only has Thermon been positively identified, as has been already mentioned, but Vlocho has been shown by an inscription found by Soteiriades to be the acropolis of the Thestiæi, a merely tribal gathering place. This solution is a surprise, a sort of anticlimax. It is an equally great surprise that Thermon had no acropolis at all, but was a gathering-place in a plain. Its situation, however, high up above the mountainous north shore of Lake Trichonis near its eastern end, made it difficult for an enemy to attack; and when Philip V. broke into the nest of the robber brood, destroyed it, and got safely back to his connections, it was the master stroke of that enterprising and rash boy king. The Ætolians got a sweet revenge more than twenty years later, when, at Kynoskephalæ, they contributed materially to Philip's crushing defeat by Flamininus.

The usual approach to Thermon is from Agrinion over a level road along the north shore until the middle of that shore-line is reached. Then comes a steady climb until one gains an altitude of perhaps two thousand feet, directly over the surface of the lake, and then another more gentle climb away from the lake, and the goal is reached. There is a fine carriage-road all the way.

The one thing that Ætolia, as well as Acarnania, lacks to make it famous is the bard, or, failing him, the historian. No Homer or Sophocles or Pindar has made the beautiful Lake Trichonis into a more than earthly lake. The great historians have found elsewhere more attractive themes than the wars of the men who inhabited these mighty fortresses. The modern traveller likes to follow the footsteps of the poets and historians; and so Attica, Argos, Bœotia, and Thessaly are visited and enjoyed, while the stream passes by Ætolia and Acarnania "on the other side." But there are some who will be drawn by that beautiful Lake Trichonis, by the bountiful Acheloos, by the Gulf of Ambrakia, and by the Gorge of Klissoura, which runs through Mount Arakynthos, and only lacks a stream to make it surpass Tempe. This number may increase so that in ten years more, demand creating supply, even Arta may provide an inn where the weary traveller may lie down to pleasant dreams.

THERMOPYLÆ

We twelve members of the American School had spent three rather cold and rainy November days at Delphi, managing to see between the showers, perhaps better called tempests, that kept sweeping up the valley of the Pleistos, most of the important objects both in the museum and in the excavation area. After so much tantalizing promise, followed by disappointment, it began to seem very doubtful whether the six bicyclists of the party could carry out their intention of prolonging the trip into Thessaly. The morning of the fourth day looked about like the three preceding mornings, except that the storm centre, on and around Mount Korax to the west of Parnassus and Delphi, had at last broken up. Just this little encouragement led five of us to move on, and we slipped quickly down the long winding road to the foot of the high slope on the top of which Delphi stands.

After we had toiled through mud to Amphissa, we began to reap the benefits of a clearing and bracing north wind. We had an exhilarating climb of three hours up the Amblema Pass, which leads over the ridge connecting Parnassus with the still higher mountains to the west. Before we got to the top, which is the backbone between the Corinthian Gulf and the Gulf of Malis, a cold cloud, which we may as well call a winter storm, came rushing out of the gap to meet us like an army debouching from a covert. We began to fear that Doris, into which we were going to pass, was another storm centre, and our feeling of pity for the one man who had been prudent enough to take his bicycle back to Athens began to change to envy. But after dropping a thousand feet or more into Doris we got below the storm, and the roads became somewhat drier. When we were at the level of that upland plain they were quite good. Doris had been a storm centre in the morning, but at noon was almost clear. What luck!

Confronting us on the north side of the plain was another mountain barrier which shut out Thermopylæ from our view. Rain-clouds were playing around this mountain. After luncheon at Gravia, it was a matter of from two to three hours to get across the plain and partly climb and partly circumvent this second barrier. And then came a most exhilarating experience. Here was the sight of a lifetime. The Gulf of Malis far below us, the road visible in all its extent winding like an enormous serpent down the side of the mountain to the plain from two to three thousand feet below us, and then running straight as an arrow to Lamia, Mount Othrys in the background, Thermopylæ to the right, and, soon after, Tymphrestos to the left, with the Spercheios winding down from it. Historic associations apart—as if they ever could be apart!—this is a landscape not easily surpassed. It is one of those views which seem to gain in power with repetition. It was the fifth time that I had seen and felt it; and I firmly believe that I had a keener relish in the view than my companions who saw it for the first time.

Bicycling down the face of a mountain like that, over curves that take you half a mile or a mile in one direction, and then as far in the other direction, is about the nearest approach to flying that has yet been given to man. One seems to be floating in the ether, and dropping at will down to the earth like a bird on the wing.

In this winding down the mountain-side we crossed probably more than once the path by which the Greek traitor led Hydarnes and his Ten Thousand Immortals around in the rear of the Greeks and cut off their retreat. But it was getting too late now to see and study Thermopylæ by the light of that day. Lamia was our goal, a city where one finds comfortable quarters and good eating. We had heard far back on the road that the bridge over the Spercheios had been carried away two years before, and had not yet been replaced. Some said that we should find a boat to ferry us over, while others said that there was neither bridge nor ferry, which seemed incredible, since we were on the great highway from the Corinthian Gulf to northern Greece. But when we reached the Spercheios at twenty minutes before five o'clock the worst that had been told us came true. No ferry-man was there. One sorrowful-looking Greek who was, figuratively speaking, in the same boat with us, suggested that we go back to a village called Moschochori, which we had passed about two miles back, the road leaving it about a quarter of a mile to the east. He thought that we should there find the ferry-man, who had abandoned his post a little too early, and had left his boat in plain sight bound to a tree with chain and padlock. This suggestion had the advantage that, in case we failed to find the boatman and to induce him to return, we might at least find shelter in the village, poor as it was, which would in the cold weather be better than passing the night in the open air.

I had on two former occasions failed to reach Lamia at nightfall and been obliged to pass the night in this region; once in 1890, very near where we were then standing, in a barn filled with corn-husks, and again, ten years later, under the hospitable roof of the chief of police at Molo, to the east of Thermopylæ. But this time it seemed as if, with a sufficient outlay of energy, we ought to pass over Jordan into a land of milk and honey. The first step was to go back. Just where we were turning from the high-road to go into the village there met us a man on horseback, who proved to be the village doctor going to visit a sick woman. The husband of the patient was trotting along behind him. No sooner did the doctor hear our story than he turned to the man following him, and said: "Go into the village and tell the ferry-man that if he doesn't get back to the ferry as fast as his legs can carry him I will split his head for him. Tell him there are strangers waiting to get over to Lamia." The word "stranger" has great power in Greece. If the stranger is not, as in Homer, under the special protection of Zeus, he is under the protection of all good men, which is perhaps quite as efficient.

At this point came a curious turn. The man who was to call the ferry-man said: "But the ferry-man will not believe me when I tell him that strangers are waiting." The doctor saw the point, and said: "Yes, one of you must go with him." I decided that I was needed, and after a hard tramp quite a distance through mud about a foot deep—I would not abate one tittle of nine inches—I saw the effect of the message. The ferry-man saddled a horse and shot off in the direction of the missing bridge as if he believed the doctor was ready to do what he had said he would do. When we reached the ferry all was in readiness for our passage, and, shortly after seven o'clock we sat down to dinner in Lamia. As the doctor and his follower went over in the same ferry-boat it is a fair inference that they had also a personal interest in stirring up the ferry-man.

The fact that this bridge had been lacking for two years on the only high-road which leads directly from Thessaly, not only to the Corinthian Gulf, but also, by a fork in Doris, to Bœotia and Attica, is a sign of the times. The people of Lamia complain against the Government, for this is a national road made and neglected by the general Government. Incomplete in 1890 when I first went over it on foot, it was completed at great expense, and it seems reckless extravagance to neglect it now. Greece might better afford to spare on its army and navy, and put the savings into internal improvements. The bridge over the Peneios, on the high-road between Trikkala and Larisa, the two principal cities of Thessaly, has been down for eight or ten years and its place has been supplied by a ferry-boat. The long-projected railroad, designed to connect Athens with Larisa, and ultimately with Europe, was nearly half finished in 1894, and until 1902 nothing was done to carry on the work, or to save from disintegration the part already finished. After a lapse of eight years a new company has taken up the work and is vigorously pushing it; but the old material has been declared to be of no value. A sense of waste in such matters makes one feel that Greece is far from being a Switzerland in thrift. It hardly affords a basis upon which a "greater Greece" can be built up.

The next day we took Thermopylæ at our leisure, passing out from Lamia over the Spercheios on the bridge of Alamana, at which Diakos, famous in ballad, resisted with a small band a Turkish army, until he was at last captured and taken to Lamia to be impaled. Luckily this one bridge over the Spercheios remains, and Thessaly has a road open to the east through Thermopylæ and Atalante. The day was perfect, a day to make an old man young. We were like boys at play, in spite of the overpowering associations of the place. We sat down in the sunlight and dabbled with our feet in the hot sulphur stream, which has given its name to the place, Thermopylæ meaning "Hot Gates," and when a serious shepherd came and looked at us in wonderment we regarded him as the "Old Man of Thermopylæ," in that character-sketch, "There was an old man of Thermopylæ who never did anything properly." We had him photographed in that character, and fancied him doomed to return for a space to the scene of his excesses and to behave himself "properly." We then went through the pass as far east as Molo, and after taking luncheon there returned to the pass for serious study, *i.e.*, for tracing as far as possible the position and movements of the antagonists in the great battle.

It may be taken as a well-known fact that the Spercheios has since the time of Herodotus made so large an alluvial deposit around its mouth that, if he himself should return to earth, he would hardly recognize the spot which he has described so minutely. The western horn, which in his time came down so near to the gulf as to leave space for a single carriage-road only, is now separated from it by more than a mile of plain. Each visit to Thermopylæ has, however, deepened my conviction that Herodotus exaggerated the impregnability of this pass. The mountain spur which formed it did not rise so abruptly from the sea as to form an impassable barrier to the advance of a determined antagonist. It is of course difficult ground to operate on, but certainly not impossible. The other narrow place, nearly two miles to the east of this, is still more open, a fact that is to be emphasized, because many topographers, including Colonel Leake, hold that the battle actually took place there, as the great battle between the Romans and Antiochos certainly did. This eastern pass is, to be sure, no place where "a thousand may well be stopped by three," and there cannot have taken place any great transformation here since classical times, inasmuch as this region is practically out of reach of the Spercheios, and the deposit from the hot sulphur streams, which has so broadened the theatre-shaped area enclosed by the two horns, can hardly have contributed to changing the shape of the eastern horn itself. Artificial fortification was always needed here; but it is very uncertain whether any of the stones that still remain can be claimed as parts of such fortification. It is a fine position for an inferior force to choose for defence against a superior one; but while it cannot be declared with absolute certainty that this is not the place where the fighting took place, yet the western pass fits better the description of Herodotus. Besides this, if the western pass had been abandoned to the Persians at the outset the fact would have been worth mentioning.

THERMOPYLÆ. FROM THE WEST

As to the heroic deed itself, the view that Leonidas threw away his own life and that of the four thousand, that it was magnificent but not strategy, not war, does not take into account the fact that Sparta had for nearly half a century been looked to as the military leader of Greece. It was audacious in the Athenians to fight the battle of Marathon without them, and they did so only because the Spartans did not come at their call. Sparta had not come to Thermopylæ in force, it is true; but her king was there with three hundred of her best men. Only by staying and fighting could he show that Sparta held by right the place she had won. It had to be done. "So the glory of Sparta was not blotted out." Had Sparta shown the white feather here, and a retreat would have been interpreted as showing the white feather, she would have lost prestige with the rest of the Greeks; and in that case it is as good as certain that Platæa would never have been fought. But besides showing the high statecraft which the occasion demanded, Leonidas was performing the simple duty of obedience to Spartan law, not to retreat before an enemy. He had been sent to hold the post; and he stayed to the end; and there is no more stirring clarion note in all that high-pitched story of the Persian war in Herodotus than the epitaph inscribed on the monument to the fallen Spartans, "Stranger, tell the Lacedemonians that we lie here in obedience to their laws." Whether Simonides felt the need of simplicity and brevity, or whether Spartan taste prescribed it, it is at any rate most fitting that boasting is omitted. The deed was so great that one little note of brag, or even some little amplifying and embellishing, would have belittled it. It is stirring to read those other equally brief and equally simple lines of Simonides inscribed on the monument erected for the total number who fought and fell: "Four thousand from Peloponnesus fought here with three millions."

One may have read, and read often, the description of the battle in the school-room, but he reads it with different eyes on the spot, when he can look up at the hillock crowned with a ruined cavalry barrack just inside the western pass and say to himself: "Here on this hill they fought their last fight and fell to the last man. Here once stood the monuments to Leonidas, to the three hundred, and to the four thousand."

The very monuments have crumbled to dust, but the great deed lives on. We rode back to Lamia under the spell of it. It was as if we had been in church and been held by a great preacher who knows how to touch the deepest chords of the heart. Eubœa was already dark blue, while the sky above it was shaded from pink to purple. Tymphrestos in the west was bathed in the light of the sun that had gone down behind it. The whole surrounding was most stirring, and there was ever sounding in our hearts that deep bass note, "What they *did* here." Even when we were afterward enjoying the great walls of the Acropolis of Pharsalos and the Vale of Tempe we kept thinking of Thermopylæ.

THESSALY

Thessaly is in a certain sense a land apart from the rest of Greece. It was so in antiquity. In spite of being the home of Jason, of Achilles, and of Alcestis, and in spite of the fact that "snowy Olympus," the home of the Greek gods, looked down upon it, the stream of its history flowed apart. In the Persian war it was prevented by force from taking any honorable part; but in the Peloponnesian war, which called all the rest of Greece to arms and divided it into two camps, it willingly stood aloof. The same may be said of most of the smaller wars which followed the Peloponnesian war. Once only did it appear that it was going to take a part, and indeed a leading part, in the affairs of Greece. But the assassination of Jason of Pheræ, who seemed about to play the rôle afterward played by the Macedonians, sent Thessaly again on her separate way.

To-day also Thessaly is a land apart. When the Kingdom of Greece was established by the European Powers Thessaly was not included in it. After it had become a part of the kingdom in 1880 it again fell into the hands of the Turks in the disastrous war of 1897, living through two sad years of subjection which were not shared by the rest of Greece. It has also suffered isolation from the rest of Greece in that while the network of railroads constantly extending out from Athens has already taken in most of Peloponnesus, and even Ætolia, it has not yet been extended to Thessaly. To reach it one must make a voyage by sea.

But this very isolation has always been to the enthusiastic traveller an added charm. Inaccessibility adds interest. The usual approach is by steamer from Piræus, and requires, according to the timetable, twenty-four hours; but it actually varies from twenty-four to forty-eight hours, according to the weather and the amount of freight to be handled on the way. The journey in itself is so charming that one need not chafe at delay, and might well prefer this method of approach even after railroad communication has been established. Particularly fine is the long stretch between Eubœa and the mainland, where mountain succeeds mountain, with Thermopylæ thrown in.

The end of the journey is the finest part of it, if one has the good fortune to enter the great Bay of Volo, called in ancient times the Gulf of Pagasæ, by daylight and in the winter. Taking associations and everything into account, there are few finer sights in the world than that which here presents itself. In front of you is Olympus, majestic, towering above the low range that separates the territory of Volo from the great basin of Thessaly. So near does it seem that one hardly thinks of it as being beyond the northern border, over in Turkey. The long ridge of Pelion is close at hand on the right, with its twenty-four villages, covered on the occasion of one of my winter visits by twelve or fourteen feet of snow, so that they abandoned for a week all attempts at communicating with one another. What Pelion lacks in height it makes up in length, and its bulk is great. It seems a strange thought of Homer to make the giants pile Pelion upon Ossa, which is a shapely and rather sharp cone. Vergil seems to do even worse in making them put Olympus on the top of the pile. Can it be that both poets made the attempt to pile the mass of Olympus or Pelion on top of the pointed Ossa a part of the daring deed? Either Olympus or Pelion would be the natural base on which to pile up the other mountains. By turning around and looking astern one sees Parnassus, which in ordinary company would absorb attention, but is here dwarfed by the sight of Olympus. In such company Othrys, on our left, hardly counts at all.

The near view with its associations claims attention. Here in the middle of Volo is the site of Iolkos, from which the Argonauts sailed out through this very bay into the distant Euxine on their daring quest. To the left are the massive walls of Pagasæ, which in classical times controlled the region. To the right is the still later controller of the bay, Demetrias, founded by the Macedonian Demetrios Polyorketes to be with Chalkis and Corinth one of the "fetters of Greece."

On my second visit to this region, which, by an unexpected chance, was only about a month after my first, having had occasion—a not unusual thing in Greece—to wait all the afternoon for a return steamer to Athens, I had a boatman named Leonidas, from Sparta, too, row me out to Demetrias, from which I got, as I then supposed, my last view on earth of Olympus. I then floated aimlessly about the bay until sunset, steeped in sunshine and mythological associations. I was so much "in the spirit" that I could almost see the centaurs prancing along the slopes of Pelion. Leonidas also seemed to enter into the spirit of the thing, and to become quite sympathetic, even if we did not or could not talk much. When I said to him, "Leonidas, do you know that the gods used to live around here?" he said, "Yes, yes," with apparent enthusiasm. I suspected, however, afterward that his enthusiasm was only skin deep, and that his chief pleasure in the affair was that he was getting pay for a whole afternoon's work without really doing much. I, on my part, was satisfied to squander on him the munificent sum of sixty cents for giving me the setting to such pleasant day-dreaming.

I am not going to recount my successive visits to Thessaly, but only to recall certain vivid impressions. I have twice entered it on the southwest, from Lamia over the passes of Othrys, and once on the northwest over the Zygos pass in the great Pindos range, and it is difficult to say which is the most impressive approach, one of these or the usual one through the Bay of Volo. Wherever you look down into the great basin from any part of the rim of mountains surrounding it, or look back at this rim from any part of the plain, you are impressed with the beauty of the plain and its surroundings.

On my first visit—how vivid are first impressions!—I came by the usual route with a companion who was in a hurry. He had an imperative engagement before him. We had a schedule to keep, and every hour was important. It was the only time that I have done Thessaly by schedule. Work on the Larisa Railroad was being pushed, and we unloaded so much material for that work at Chalkis that we did not get off until afternoon, and, at Stylidha, the port of Lamia, we kept unloading until after midnight. The result was that we did not reach Volo until the next morning, over twelve hours behind time. By a dash for the station we secured the first train, and reached Larisa at about ten o'clock. Thessaly has had since 1884 its own very good railroad system, starting from Volo and branching at Velestino, the ancient Pheræ, one branch going to Larisa and the other to Trikkala and beyond. This system connects the three principal cities, Volo, Larisa, and Trikkala, each of about fifteen thousand inhabitants, and brings the traveller near to all the interesting points of the land.

In order to carry out our schedule it was necessary for us to see the Vale of Tempe that day. Without losing a minute we engaged our carriage at the station, a mile from the town, and drove through the town, where we gathered a little stock of provisions while the driver changed horses. Of course, he had told us that our scheme was impossible, but we forced him along. In spite of mud (it was March, and Thessaly is always muddy at that time), we got through Tempe, and came back, reaching Larisa before nine o'clock in the evening. Without a full moon it would have been impossible to do Tempe that day. On that evening we caught for the first time the notes of the Greek frogs, *Brek-ke-ke-kek-koak-koak*, reproducing Aristophanes with the exception of a few sibilants.

Tempe is one of the two great show pieces of Thessaly. Even the ancients, who are often said to have set little store by beauties of nature, were enthusiastic over Tempe, although they appear to have paid little attention to the other great show piece, the cliffs of Meteora. Herodotus records that Xerxes was struck with wonder at the great defile five miles long with steep sides and a mighty river, the Peneios, flowing through it. One fine feature of Tempe is also the view which one gets at the end, out over the sea to the site of Potidæa and Olynthos.

The Thessalian legend that Poseidon split open with his trident the great eastern range of mountain, and let out here between Ossa and Olympus the water which had made Thessaly a lake, is strictly true if we let the trident represent earthquake force. Geology accepts the legend in all its essential features. Thessaly was until comparatively late times, geologically speaking, a lake. It is now a lake bottom of inexhaustible fertility.

The next day, instead of taking the train back to Pheræ and over the other branch which we were going to traverse later, we took a carriage to drive straight across due west to Trikkala, intending to take the train there for the last fourteen miles of the journey to Kalabaka, which lies at the foot of the Meteora cliffs. We were off at six o'clock, and had over eight hours for our drive of thirty-seven miles. When we had done two-thirds of it the driver stopped to bait his horses. He knew that we had taken him expressly to bring us to Trikkala in season to catch the train, and yet he waited so long that it became very doubtful by the time he was ready to start whether we could do it. We offered five drachmas extra if he did it; and he tried hard to get them then, whipping his horses unmercifully. The result was that we saw the train go out of the station as we got into the outskirts of the town.

The horses were unable to make the extra fourteen miles to Kalabaka that night, and an essential part of our schedule was to spend the night at one of the monasteries perched upon the picturesque rocks. We must spend that very night there or give up the plan entirely. Our driver tried in vain to get other horses for us. One man promised to come with a carriage in half an hour, and at the end of that time came and said that he could not go, the road was too bad. From subsequent experience I judge that he was right. Somebody in the crowd of interested bystanders suggested that we take a hand-car, which the station-agent could give us by telegraphing to Volo for authorization to do so. When we went to the station-agent with our plan, we judged by his answer that our advisers had been mildly guying us. By this time quite a crowd had gathered, curious to see what we would do next.

We now gave an unexpected turn to events by picking up our heels and our very small packs and starting off along the railroad track, at a good athletic pace for Kalabaka. Probably the crowd expected to see us come back and lodge at Trikkala; but we reached Kalabaka in three hours and a half, at nearly eight o'clock. Hungry and tired, we sat down in an eating-house and began our supper with the feeling that we had missed our game, except in so far as we had got sight of the wonderful rocks which towered high up above the village. What we had wanted was the sensation of passing the night on top of one of these needles. When our desire was made known it seemed as if everybody in the village was determined that we should get into the monastery that night. Some went and brought the astynomos (chief of gendarmes), and he promptly detailed two of his men to escort us up; and as soon as we had eaten we set off. Again the full moon saved us. Without it it would have been impossible to scale the heights, even with the best of guides. There was some incidental gain in the view afforded by moonlight. One enormous round tower, about fifty times as large as the famous Heidelberg

Tower, has never looked to me by daylight as impressive as it did then by moonlight.

When at last we came to the bridge which spanned the chasm separating the cliff on which stood the monastery of St. Stephen from the body of the mountain our attendants shouted and cracked their whips over the reverberating chasm until a sleepy monk put his head out of a window in a third story and said, in a sleepy voice: "What time is it now?" On being told that it was ten o'clock he seemed disinclined to admit our claim, which the gendarmes urged vehemently. We made out that the gist of the claim was that here were strangers who had come all the way from America, ten thousand miles away, just to see that monastery. Suddenly the parleying was stopped by the shutting of the window. We thought that we were shut out; but the gendarmes lingered as if they thought their appeal had taken effect; and, in fact, after a delay of several minutes, which seemed to us much longer, we heard the clapping of wooden soles along the stone flagging inside the oaken door, which was soon after swung open. We went to sleep that night congratulating ourselves on having restored by our own good legs, aided by a kind full moon, a programme that had been broken by a shiftless driver.

The next morning, after climbing up St. Trinity by means of a series of ladders arranged in a cleft of the rock, we caught the train which took us to Pharsala at noon. From there we walked to Domoko, since made famous by the stand made by the Greek army in the war of 1897, and called in ancient times Thaumakoi, "the wonderful," on account of the superb view of the great plain of Thessaly which it affords. On the following day we reached the port of Lamia, slightly stiff from the bare tables on which we had slept at Domoko, and there ended our Thessalian trip.

The Meteora (literally "aloft") cloisters can hardly be enough praised. There were once twenty-four of them, all perched upon these needles. They were placed there in the fourteenth century for the sake of security from robber bands. Only about a half-dozen of them are now occupied; the rest are wholly or partly ruined. St. Stephen is the only one that regularly entertains guests. Two of the most difficult to ascend, the Meteoron and St. Barlaam, are more than a mile away from St. Stephen; and an ascent of these is not easily combined with spending the night at St. Stephen, unless one spends there all the next day and night also. On a later visit I made the really perilous ascent of the Meteoron on a series of ladders dangling along the perpendicular face of the needle, 1,820 feet above the sea-level, and, at a rough estimate, 200 feet above the flat rock from which you start to climb. When I had once gone up and walked about a little I shrank from the descent. I was particularly nervous when I started downward by backing out of the window, and holding on to the sill with my hands, while I felt for the rounds of the ladder below with my feet. I felt then that, as never before, I had taken my life into my hands. When we asked the monks why they had refused to wind us up in the basket with which they hauled up their fuel and supplies, they replied that there were so few of them that they were afraid that their strength would give out while they had us in mid-air. This explanation satisfied us completely. One would rather trust to his own hands and feet than to an insufficient force of monks. But since the least failure of one's own hands or feet meant certain death, one is satisfied by having made the ascent once, and having experienced a sensation.

METEORA MONASTERIES

At St. Stephen the hospitality is most cheerfully accorded, and nothing exacted in return; but one usually puts something into "the box," as an expression of thankfulness. The monasteries are all rich landed proprietors and need not our poor alms. I recall one occasion when their hospitality was more bountiful than timely. Professor Edward Capps and I once arrived at St. Stephen with our wives at six o'clock, in a state bordering on starvation. We immediately heard a clattering of dishes below stairs, and pretty soon an exhalation of savory odors began to rise from the kitchen. From time to time a monk would bring up a pitcher or a plate, while we endured the pains of Tantalus until half-past nine, simply because our hosts wanted to do something extra, regarding the presence of ladies as making an extraordinary occasion. A little cold meat and bread at six o'clock would have been more keenly appreciated by us than the eight courses with which they finally plied us. Let the traveller in Greece beware of special occasions.

My last three visits to Thessaly have been made by bicycle. One gets over the ground more rapidly that way. For example, in February, 1900, Mr. Benjamin Powell and I rode from Trikkala to Larisa in two hours and thirty-seven minutes, including a short delay at the ferry over the Peneios. Baedeker puts this journey as "37 miles, 8 hours, carriage about 50 drachmas." We had time in the afternoon of the same day to go out to Tempe and back without trespassing much upon the evening. Sometimes, however, the tale is not so triumphant. In February, 1902, five of us were doing this same journey at a somewhat more gentle gait, and, just after remounting from the ferry, ran over some particularly dry and stiff Thessalian thistles, reducing about half of our tires to the condition of sieves in a few seconds. A long and pensive walk into Larisa was the penalty imposed on three of the party; and we took a carriage out to Tempe the next day.

Sometimes one in travelling blunders into a good thing. Before the journey just mentioned I had several times passed Pharsala with just pause enough to take in the probable topography of the great battle between Cæsar and Pompey, and once only had I taken a rather hasty view of the walls of the acropolis. But this time, by the chance of two of our party lagging behind on the descent from Domoko, we missed a train that we might have taken to carry us a long way on toward Kalabaka. When I realized that we were compelled to pass the night at Pharsala, I expected to "pay of my person," inasmuch as we had no guest friend to fall back upon. What was my surprise to find a perfectly clean hotel opened only fourteen months before, bearing the name of the patriot poet, Rhegas Pheræos. We were in luck.

But greater luck it was that we had a half-day to explore carefully the walls of the acropolis. Some parts of these are seen to be as old as those of Mycenæ. Some think that here was the home of Achilles. If this is so, he had a citadel that might vie with that of his chief. In the midst of our study of walls we were from time to time impelled to look up to majestic Olympus, and also to look into the deep cut between it and Ossa, the Vale of Tempe, through which Pompey, up to that time so fortunate, but then a broken man, fled precipitate to his doom.

AN ASCENT OF THE HIGHEST MOUNTAIN IN GREECE

Probably if the question which is the highest mountain in Greece were proposed to a lot of candidates for admission to college, whose equipment in Greek geography is better than it is likely to be at any other time, the majority of the suffrages would go to either Olympus or Parnassus. But Olympus, with all its Greek associations, is, alas! a mountain in Turkey; and as for Parnassus, it is overtopped by nearly two hundred feet by a mountain to the west of it. This mountain, called Kiona, a part of the group known in antiquity under the name of Korax, "Crow Mountain," has the honor of being the highest mountain in the Kingdom of Greece. Parnassus, to be sure, by the greatness of its fame more than overcomes the lacking two hundred feet, just as Erymanthus, on account largely of its famous boar, is of more importance than its higher neighbor to the east, Aroania. But there are always a few spirits who wish to scale the highest heights.

The American School at Athens has, in the various persons representing it, scaled most of the mountains of Greece; but not until 1898 had it scaled the highest. We had hoped to do it with a considerable force; but late in June the men get scattered. There remained but four of us together at the close of the campaign in Corinth. When I told the Government Ephor, attendant upon our work, that we proposed to shake off the dust of our excavations by climbing Kiona, he developed a sudden interest in my welfare, and begged me not to venture it, or at least to take along a posse of soldiers. When I said that I had climbed most of the mountains of Greece without harm or fear, he said that this particular part of Greece, Ætolia, and at this particular time, was dangerous. The men of that section were, he said, particularly bad men. I had so often heard men of other villages and sections called in the lump bad men, when they in reality proved no worse than those who gave them that bad name, that I was not shaken until our overseer also, an intelligent man, begged me not to go. He said that the shepherds of Kiona were a bad lot and known as such all over Greece. I did not so much mind taking my own life in my hand, but felt some scruple about hazarding that of my fourteen-year-old boy, whose party it really was. So when we awoke at midnight at New Corinth to find that the boat which was to take us to Itea had, after the manner of Greek boats, gone through the canal without turning toward Corinth at all, I proposed that, taking this as a sort of "judgment of God," we should return to Athens. But others of the party said that they felt ashamed to give up an enterprise that had been so much talked about. So, considering ourselves a sort of society with an object, we did not dissolve. We had lost one day; but, taking the west-bound train to Ægion, which we reached at two o'clock in the afternoon, with a delay of only fifteen minutes we were aboard a sail-boat with a stern wind driving us toward Itea, which the boatmen promised to reach in three hours. But promises based upon wind are rarely kept. We were, it is true, nearly at the mouth of the Bay of Itea, perhaps four-fifths of the way, at the end of three hours. But then the wind fell, and much rowing followed, at which we all took a hand. And it was nearly eleven o'clock when we reached Itea.

We had hoped to reach Amphissa, seven miles from Itea, and then make our arrangements for climbing the mountain before going to sleep. But now all we could do was to avoid sleeping at Itea, which we did by walking about half a mile, and ascending a little knoll where we spread our blankets and slept under the open sky. It was not hard to get up at four o'clock the next morning and reach Amphissa shortly after six. By the time we had made a scanty breakfast horses were engaged for two days; and while they were being made ready we had an hour to devote to the remains of ancient Amphissa, on which Philip's heavy hand fell as a preliminary to the battle of Chæronea. There is one gate here that is one of the finest specimens of Greek fortification extant, the sight of which made me realize what an oversight I had been guilty of eight years ago, when I passed by this acropolis as a mediæval affair.

Nobody in this town of over five thousand inhabitants appeared to have the local knowledge that fitted him to be our guide; and so we set out with the understanding that at a monastery three hours up we should find such a man. When we reached the monastery it was high noon, and hot, as became the fifteenth of June. The solitary monk, Chrysanthos Liaskos, upbraided us for not telling him that we were coming, that he might have killed for us a lamb, or at least some chickens. But how little we knew just when we were coming! Such as he had he gave us, and refused payment.

The old wall paintings in his chapel, some of them four or five hundred years old, were very fine, but were now rapidly going to ruin with the crumbling walls. His face lighted up as he told us of miracles performed in this chapel, not hundreds of years ago, but last year and under his own eyes. He was a very wide-awake man, and appeared to be convinced of the truth of his own story.

The best thing he did for us was to get from the neighboring village, Sigritza, a very competent guide. When we got off at half-past two, the horses, which went only about two hours farther, were serviceable mainly in carrying our packs. After that our guide led us over difficult foot-paths which climbed along the edges of precipices and up heights only to descend again. We proceeded more rapidly now that we had got rid of our slow-paced horses, which were to return to the monastery and come to meet us the next morning. At nightfall we came to a hut at the foot of the main peak, which required an hour and a half of climbing in the morning. We received the warmest welcome from shepherds who were friends and relations of our guide. They did not seem at all like the dreadful men of whom we had been forewarned. They made a most savory brew of half a kid—but the milk! Only from such pastures can such milk come. We all regretted engagements that prevented our staying a week, that we might do justice to this mountain dairy.

It was half-past ten before we could go to rest. Then the shepherds took us to a cave where they kept their cheeses, which gave just room enough to pack us in. They then closed the door with boughs and a big stone to keep out the cold night wind and the dogs. We had just time to note how much our lodging seemed like the cave of Polyphemos in the Odyssey, and get a good whiff of the cheese, when, with apparently no interval at all, we heard our guide calling out that it was time to get up and be off. Where the heart of that night went to I never knew.

When, at four o'clock, we had finished our toil, we got a great reward. The view was the finest that I had had in Greece. Both the Corinthian Gulf and Thermopylæ seemed to lie at our feet. The sun soon rose in line with the strait between Eubœa and Thessaly, making that strait, with Skopelos and Skiathos blocking its exit, a sea of fire. To the south was the great trio of Arcadian mountains; to the northeast, closing a long line of mountains beginning with Pelion, was the majestic Olympus; to the northwest stood Tymphrestos, in lonely dignity; while to the west, peak upon peak and chain upon chain of Ætolia made a most bewildering impression. On the whole it was a panorama that can never fade from the mind's eye. Two years earlier, in climbing Parnassus, I had been defrauded by clouds of all that was best in this view, viz., that to the north and east.

When we got back to the shepherds' quarters and began our farther descent at seven o'clock, I gave the head man two five-drachma pieces, as a slight reward for what they had done for us. He seemed perplexed, and at last gave me back one of the pieces, and asked me if I could change it, as I had given him too much. You may believe that I didn't do it. And I couldn't help smiling to think how carefully I had hidden away my watch in my trousers pocket, for fear that the gold chain might tempt these bad men. Of all the gentle shepherds whom I have met on Greek mountains, these were the gentlest and best.

From the glorious mountain air and cold water, trickling down over precipices a thousand feet high, we came at evening again to Amphissa, with its stifling air and scanty water-supply, and, worst of all, with its one hotel, which has not improved since 1890. It is a fact that there was only one wash-basin in the house, and it was very hard to get a turn at it. Our sufferings in the night were dreadful; and when in the morning the landlord tried to persuade us that they were caused by mosquitoes, the meekest man in our party got angry almost to the point of profanity, and pointed out blood-stains on the sheets that were evidently not those of mosquitoes. And yet this landlord tried to do well by us, giving us four of his six beds, while well-dressed Greeks slept on his dining-tables. But stop! Perhaps they knew better than we what they were about. If one were shut up to a choice between Itea and Amphissa for a night's lodging, it would be better to take to the woods, especially in summer. And during that long summer night of torture we regretted that we were not lying again in the open field on our blankets.

But regrets are out of place, and nothing but the pleasure remains when one thinks of the glories of Kiona.

A JOURNEY FROM ATHENS TO ERETRIA

Most hand-books of travel in Greece, beginning with the invaluable Baedeker, impress it upon their readers that there are no long distances in Greece. Even without the help of railroads, which, of course, as far as they extend, have annihilated the barriers between the old "jarring states," one finds the historic places, like Corinth, Delphi, Chæronea, Thebes, and many others lying so near one another that, after lodging in one of them, one can always count on spending the next night at another. One loses no time. On the map, according to which one might lay out a scheme of travel, Athens and Eretria lie very near together. The overland route to Oropos, with a short sail across the Eubœan Gulf, can be compassed in any summer's day. But the surest and most convenient way is supposed to be to take the steamer at Piræus in the early evening, and wake at Chalkis the next morning, and take a ride of three hours to Eretria in the morning air. But this simple and easy scheme sometimes fails in practice, as my experience has shown.

On Wednesday, February 18, 1891, three of us started out from Piræus at evening to re-enforce one student of the American School who, in very bad weather, had been carrying on excavations begun several weeks before. We had deferred sailing for three days on account of the weather. As we set out it was a grief to us that we must sail past Sunion, Marathon, and Rhamnus before daybreak. We wished to supplement previous acquaintance with those places by a view from the sea. The night wore away with considerable tossing, and in order to get a little view of the narrowing Euripos at Chalkis I arose at half-past six. Seeing that we were near land on the left, I asked a sailor what land it was, and got for an answer something that sounded like "Macaroni." Not remembering any such land in the neighborhood of Chalkis, I cleared my eyes, looked about me, and became sharply interrogative. Now I elicited the well-known name "Sunion." This was astounding. Leaning far out over the railing I saw the columns crowning the "steep." Ah! good fortune was going to allow us to see Marathon by broad daylight.

It did not take long to see that we were in a boisterous sea. My various Atlantic experiences furnished no parallel to it. Not only were the billows high, but the fierce northeast wind, mingled with sleet, seemed to take up the tops of them and carry them up into the sky. It required two hours more for us to round the point of Sunion. It was a great effort for the good ship Peneios, and when that was accomplished we seemed to come to nothing better, and we were soon aware of the determination of our level-headed captain to put into the harbor of Laurion from stress of weather.

All that day and the next day we lay in that harbor, if it can be called lying to roll about as we did. The long island, Makronisi, called in antiquity Helene, almost makes Laurion a land-locked harbor. But between this island and the mainland the northeast wind came tearing through with unabated fury for forty-eight hours. The projection of the mainland to the north of the harbor being quite low, we were as poorly protected as it was possible to be in that harbor. Several of the vessels which had taken refuge there appeared to be having a rougher time than the Peneios. Our captain looked on with some pride when an English steamer dragged her anchor nearly across the whole width of the harbor. During the second night we had some fears of an Apia disaster. No boats went to or from the land, and so we lay the greater part of two days, unable to telegraph to our friends in Athens, as much shut off from the world as if we were on an ocean voyage. Yet nobody thought of wishing to see the captain change his mind and sail on. At last, on Saturday morning, at about two o'clock, we steamed out, and were as badly shaken at the start as one often finds it his lot to be. One lesson was most thoroughly impressed upon us, that there may have been good cause in antiquity for Athenian fleets shunning the winter trip northward, and for Philip's being allowed free hand to accomplish his undertakings Thraceward at that season of the year.

Little recked we of Marathon, or Rhamnus, or Oropos in the blinding storm in which we at last reached Chalkis, and were rowed ashore in blinding snow and splashing water from the oars. Photographic apparatus was in special danger.

Once landed we seemed near Eretria, but here our vicissitudes thickened. Between us and Basiliko, the half-way halting-place on the road to Eretria, was one of the numerous Potamos of Greece, which was taking this opportunity to justify its name, to make up for being nothing but a dry bed nine months in the year. All coach-drivers but one said that the Potamo would be as far as we could go toward Eretria that day. But this one talked so confidently of being able to find horses for us at the Potamo that we entrusted ourselves to his care, and started out in the rain.

The course lay through the famous Lelantine Plain, which, in spite of the rain, was seen to be a paradise. Such vines and fig-trees and, farther on, such grain-fields! I had not seen its like in Greece. It is no wonder that it was a bone of contention almost before the dawn of history. It is something of a testimonial to the power and ambition of Eretria that it reached so far out from its own fertile plain to grasp at what geographically belonged to Chalkis.

Our driver soon made a halt, and informed us that we were at the end of our stipulated drive. There were no signs of any river or any horses. He said the river was a quarter of a mile farther on, and that the horses were not his lookout. On being told either to find horses or drive back to Chalkis, he became surly, and demanded, besides the liberal sum of twenty drachmas which we had agreed to pay at this point, twenty drachmas more for driving us back. We told him that we should pay nothing at all except on a hearing before the demarch of Chalkis. He at last drove slowly back, going through the form of inquiring at several houses for horses, but getting none.

Arrived at Chalkis, we all went to the demarch's office, and, shivering over a pan of coals, discussed the case. Under the demarch's pacific influence, we arranged to have the same man drive us out again the next day, paying a total of thirty drachmas, and in the meantime to telegraph to the demarch of Eretria to send us horses to meet us at the river.

The next day was no better than the preceding, and we postponed starting for several hours, in hopes of a cessation of the rain. When at last we reached the river, and looked across the arches of the bridge then lying several years unfinished, though the rest of the road was ready for use, we were unable to get any response to our shouts. At last somebody told us that a man from Eretria had got tired of shouting for us an hour before, and had returned the way he came. Here was an emergency. We must go forward. After much beating about the neighborhood, one little unpromising-looking horse was found. By making trips enough we could by means of this weak creature get over to Basiliko, and then perhaps still get on to Eretria. By the aid of a long rope, our effects were soon made fast to the many-horned Greek saddle, and we started to make the quarter-mile distance to a ford a little below the bridge. Going along the top of one of the dikes thrown up to facilitate watering of the vineyards, our horse slipped and came down the bank into a foot of Lelantine mud. Our effects scattered about under him prevented his absolute disappearance. But this was bad for the effects. Some of the cargo was at last righted, and the horse ungently pulled by application of force at both ends into a standing position, and by some carrying of bags and bundles we reached the river-bank. The stalwart boy who accompanied the horse ventured into the water to test its depth. It was clear that that weak horse could not keep his footing there.

Our stalwart boy was equal to the emergency. Taking us one by one on his back he bore us over, and then the parcels, spending nearly an hour in the operation. The sight of a bearded gentleman being carried pickapack across a rushing river by a boy whose footing could not be very secure on the uneven river-bed, and who could not quite keep the boots of his rider out of the water, is a very ridiculous one to a bystander; but as each one's turn came it became a serious event to him.

When we were all well over, we noticed that the faithful horse had followed his master, and got across also. By his help we easily made the half mile to Basiliko, where our man from Eretria was still waiting for us; and that night we spent at Eretria, ready to inaugurate what proved to be most interesting and successful excavations on the site of that city on which the storm of Persian vengeance fell before it was scattered at Marathon.

We had a most unusual March. At one time snow lay on the ground a foot deep for three days. But we excavated the greater part of the ancient theatre and many interesting graves, besides mapping out the walls of the city. In subsequent years we took up the work again, and uncovered the old gymnasium and a temple of Dionysos near the theatre, but we stopped too soon; after us the Greeks took up the work, and achieved results that nearly overshadowed ours. But ours will ever be the service of having uncovered one of the most interesting theatres of Greece, and a real Greek gymnasium, which is a rare thing, inasmuch as most gymnasia which are preserved to us are Roman modifications of the original Greek form. More than this, we forever laid the idea, up to that time so prevalent, that the Eretria which was destroyed by the Persians was several miles to the east of this. The acropolis walls did that; but it was the service of the Greek excavator to uncover the temple of Apollo, with its archaic gable sculptures, and to find a considerable quantity of large vases of the sixth century before Christ, and thus to corroborate the testimony of the walls. There was, in fact, no other such place for a commanding acropolis on the whole stretch of shore as on the hill rising above the theatre. Any city established further east would have deserved the name of "the city of the blind."

TAYGETOS AND KITHÆRON

If the coupling of these two names seems forced, my first reason for it is the purely formal one that ten days after being on the summit of Taygetos, we were climbing Kithæron. Greece is such a small country that to traverse it from end to end in ten days, and see Sparta, Argos, and Thebes, with some mountain climbing thrown in, is nothing that justifies a boastful feeling; but when, at the end of such a journey, one reflects upon the history and mythology which is attached to these names, and calls up the scenes enacted on the plains on which he looks down from these mountains, he wonders at what he has accomplished.

The mountains of Greece have many and great charms; and they have this pre-eminent claim on our attention, that they are the unchanged witnesses of the past. Poor villages occupy the Cadmeia and the site of Sparta; waves of immigration have swept over Greece to such an extent that one may be in honest doubt whether the people who walk these dirty streets have any more claim to be the heirs and representatives of Leonidas and Epaminondas, whose names perchance they bear, than we have. The plains and rivers remain, except that the former have lost their trees and the latter their water. But Taygetos, "rock-ribbed and ancient as the sun," remains as it was. The great men of Greece knew the mountains, and were known of them. Alkman and Pindar had held converse with Taygetos and Kithæron, which now remain as their sole surviving companions.

Six years ago I had approached Sparta from Messenia *through* Taygetos, and had arrived at evening when the sun sent its rays almost level through the orange-trees loaded with fruit and redolent with blossoms. I feared that any different approach might bring a sort of disappointment. But when, after a morning at Mantineia, in the upland plain of Arcadia, we gained the top of the last height of the pass, and saw the long ridge of Taygetos towering before us with the sun just sinking behind it, we stood leaning over our bicycles and gave way to silence like that of "stout Cortez and his men." What went through my mind could hardly be called reflection, unless I could so designate an acceptance of the propriety of the one epithet, περιμήκετος, which Homer chose for this mighty mass, whether he intended it in the sense of "stretched out" or "high towering." Night was beginning to fall before we could break the spell and move down into the valley of the Eurotas, and it was already dark when we crossed the bridge of the Eurotas and entered Sparta. The object of this journey was not so much to visit Sparta as to climb Taygetos; but, while waiting until the afternoon of the next day for another contingent of the American School to come after us from Tripolitza by carriage, we used the time to visit the site of Amyklæ, and to hunt up the mound from which came the celebrated Vaphio cups, the finest product of the goldsmith's art left to our wondering eyes by the Achæan civilization of Greece.

SPARTA WITH TAYGETOS IN THE BACKGROUND

Taygetos is the highest mountain in Peloponnesus, outranking Kyllene by somewhat more than a hundred feet, and falling only a hundred feet short of eight thousand. Since Sparta is only slightly above the sea-level, the task before us was arduous, and when our forces were united, we decided to make a part of the ascent before evening. An acquaintance in Sparta gave me a letter of introduction to a leading man of Anavryti, a village three hours up the mountain. When we reached his house at dusk, in the middle of a village that resounded with flowing streams, this letter opened his doors and his heart. It opened the doors so wide that the neighbors came streaming in to see us, to such an extent that he was at last glad to avail himself of the help of a gendarme with his whip to clear out the younger portion of his self-invited guests. He then set to work, in the manner of Greek hosts, to kill us with kindness, making us eat and drink for about two hours. After this came those futile attempts to sleep which those who have travelled much in the interior of Greece know too well. At half-past two we were only too ready to stop the fight with the small enemy and address ourselves to the overcoming of Taygetos. For the first two hours we went on by the light of a lantern, guided by the son of our host, over a difficult path which gave us an occasional fall. After that came the gorgeous sunrise and the increasing reward in the ever more extended outlook, which made us almost forget that we had not slept. It was owing, however, largely to this lack of sleep that one of our number gave out a thousand feet below the summit, while another was with some difficulty coached over the last five hundred feet.

When we were at last on the summit at half-past ten, the reward was a perfect view—the first absolutely perfect view which I had ever had out of many mountain ascents in Greece. We had, fortunately, taken the rare moment when, after four days of cloudy and rainy weather, the sky had just cleared, and for half a day a perfectly cloudless ether was diffused over everything. We saw the valley of the Eurotas winding down from the mountains to the sea, where it empties near Helos, the "marsh town," which is said to have given its name to the whole remnant of the Achæan people, who were reduced to a galling bondage under the Dorian spearmen from the north. Sparta looked so near that we were almost lured into the attempt to throw stones into it. Kythera was surprisingly near, and even Crete—troubled and troublesome Crete—seemed so near that annexation to Greece appeared to be a most obvious lot for it. The southern islands of the Ægean, Melos and its neighbors, were conspicuous to the east; while on the west it seemed as if we could almost slide down into the Messenian Gulf. But, while all these objects caught our attention time and again, it was still to the north that our gaze was mainly directed; for there lay the whole Peloponnesus, with its peaks and ridges, which compose the greater part of it, spread out before us like a raised map, closed in on the north by the big three, Kyllene, Aroania, and Erymanthos. Compared with these, the three Attic mountains to the extreme left, and somewhat distant, looked small, though distinct. It was a place and a scene that one must needs be reluctant to leave. Had we brought food with us we should have been tempted to stay and spend the night in the substantial "tabernacle for Elias," which crowns this summit, according to the usual practice in Greece. But evening brought us to Sparta, a good many stone's-throws distant, as we felt in our knees and in our appetites. Two suggestions force themselves upon one visiting this region: the first is that the Spartans showed wonderful energy in breaking through the wall of Taygetos, and conquering their Dorian neighbors in Messenia, and in crushing them again when they made a desperate attempt to throw off the yoke; the second is that the difference between these two branches of Dorians could not be due to the Messenians having, as is sometimes alleged, settled in a fatally fertile and enervating plain. If rich fields could enervate a people, the Spartans surely did not lack that invitation, for the valley of the Eurotas must have been in antiquity, as now, a garden.

But what an unlovely people was this armed camp, which goes under the name of Sparta! We will not reproach them that they failed to produce anything in art and literature. It is rather their meanness and absolute selfishness, as the strongest military power in Greece, that makes them odious. For a century, from the Persian war to Leuctra, whenever Sparta moved through the passes to the north it meant woe to some Greek city; and when there was question raised at home over the unrighteous conduct of a general abroad, the outspoken criterion was: "Has he acted for the interests of Sparta?"

The last great injustice was the seizing and holding the Cadmeia in time of peace. It is this that makes lovers of fair play rejoice at the crushing return blow delivered by Epaminondas and his Thebans at Leuctra, and take satisfaction in his passing down the Eurotas, and showing the women of Sparta, for the first time, "the smoke of an enemy's camp." And now by a historical thread we are led from Taygetos and Sparta over to Thebes and Kithæron.

By a lucky choice we approached Thebes, not by any of the usual routes, but by taking the train from Athens to Megara, walking thence across to the east end of the Corinthian Gulf, and skirting its shore until we reached Ægosthenæ, at the foot of Kithæron. No traveller ought to neglect this region. It is one of the finest shores in Greece; so rugged that we were several times driven inland by a promontory rising perpendicularly from the sea, and made to climb more than a thousand feet before we could continue our journey. We took a recompense for the extra toil by tipping off into the sea several bowlders, some of which, striking a projecting crag, would reach the water with the effect of a bursting shell. This whole northeastern arm of the Corinthian Gulf runs in between Kithæron on the north and Geraneia on the south, and so gains a peculiar seclusion.

And Ægosthenæ! the northwestern frontier town of the Megarid, what a magnificent ruin! The view that we took of its walls and towers by the full moon was something not to be forgotten. At Ægosthenæ we were on the route so often travelled by the Spartans when they went over into Bœotia to "regulate" its affairs, and it was under these walls that the remnant of their beaten and disheartened army first stopped to take breath on getting out of Bœotian territory after Leuctra. We had planned to follow this entire route, but, since even this involved some climbing, we agreed to take a little more climbing and go in a straight line for Platæa, over the top of Kithæron, in spite of the fact that the mountain wore a cap of cloud. So, having taken a very cold sea-bath and another good look at the ruins of Ægosthenæ, which were only a little less imposing by day than by moonlight, we scaled the height with a single peasant for a guide, and his mule to carry our packs. After many a look back on the increasingly beautiful scene behind us, whenever the dark fir-trees, which cover the slopes and give the name of "fir mountain" as a substitute for the old name Kithæron, allowed it, we at last entered into the cloud just before reaching the top. In the darkness of cloud and fir-trees we better felt that we were on the mountain chosen by the Erinnyes for their abode, a place of howlings, the scene of woe for Œdipus, Actæon, Pentheus, and Agave. Who would wish for sunlight on such a spot? It would have been as inappropriate as a cloud on Taygetos. While we were musing thus, suddenly there came a rift in the cloud, and we saw the whole plain of Bœotia once, twice, three times, and the spell of the Erinnyes was broken. We went five hundred feet further down on the north side, where we seemed to have left behind us the awful myths and to have come down into the realms of history; for we were looking down into Platæa, which lay at our feet. One of the brightest pages in Greek history is the unbroken record of the heroism of Platæa, and when it was finally crushed one might well have written over it, "dead on the field of honor." Its Athenian leanings were abhorrent to Thebes, which always desired a "big Bœotia." But no one could have done a better turn to Platæa than did Thebes, when it espoused the cause of Persia and led away nearly all the rest of Bœotia with it. At the close of "old Platæa's day" the Panhellenic spirit of Platæa was rewarded by the Greeks in their giving the fine old heroic city the prize of valor, and declaring its soil forever sacred and inviolate. But the gods gave it a greater prize, in that they made its name forever associated with the battle that made Greece free.

It was again dark when we entered Thebes, and again we seemed to have left the realm of bright history and to have come under the spell of the awful myths of Cadmus's line, the horrors of Œdipus and his fratricidal sons, dark horrors relieved only by the bright form of Antigone.

STYX AND STYMPHALUS

Arcadia is a name to conjure with. It "throngs the pulses with the fulness of the spring." It had been my lot to pass twice through Southern Arcadia from east to west. But the great plains of Mantineia and Megalopolis lie open to the sunlight, and have nothing weird or even poetical about them. Even Lykosoura and Bassæ do not belong to the Arcadia that furnished the stories about singing fishes and aquatic mice. We must look elsewhere for those wonderful fountains, some of which cured madness, while one not only cured drunkenness, but, passing beyond the "touch not, taste not, handle not," made even the smell of wine forever odious. It is recorded, by the way, that somebody set up an inscription by this fountain, warning the traveller against drinking of it. All these features belong to Northern Arcadia.

Mantineia is historically the most interesting city of Arcadia; and yet I had twice looked from its walls through those deep gorges to the north, knowing that just through the first one, almost in sight, lay old Orchomenos, and longed to pass through that gateway, but had been prevented by other claims upon my time. But in the summer of 1895 I was allowed the delight of seven days in the saddle with two pleasant companions in these uplands where reality is more inspiring than the Louis Quatorze fictions that have been thrown around the name of Arcadia.

To one accustomed to arid Attica and Argolis, the abundance of water and trees in this region is most striking. The three great northern mountains look bare enough at their tops; but they reach up and draw down from the sky that store of moisture which Pentelicus and Arachnæon are impotent to procure. Everywhere about them are rippling streams lined with plane-trees, with here and there a magnificent chestnut grove, and mountains covered with forests of pine and fir. Fields of maize (with here and there a patch of hemp), watered by thousands of little streams, diverted from the brooks, remind us of home. Around Nonakris, which was almost the farthest point north reached in our journey, is a wild tangle of vegetation which makes it difficult to keep the paths, which follow along the streams, from becoming overgrown and impassable. From this tangle we snatched many luscious blackberries as we rode past, catching some briers with the berries.

Nonakris was in ruins when Pausanias visited it, but past it flowed the river Styx, the name of which is probably better known than any other Arcadian name. It was a painful and somewhat dangerous toil of about three hours from the nearest of the half-dozen villages which represent the ancient Nonakris to the foot of the famous waterfall from which the river comes down. I use the word "toil" rather than ascent, for, it being impossible to force our way up the bed of the stream, we had to climb down about half as much as up; in fact, it was, taken in the heat of noonday, a more toilsome climb than the ascent of Aroania, which we had made on the same day before daybreak.

THE STYGIAN POOL

When, after all, we stood face to face with the fall our feeling was one of disappointment. It was nearly the middle of September, and though Aroania, holding snow in its gorges all the year round, may be called with more propriety than Ætna "the nurse of snow," there was little water falling, and we saw none of the rainbow effects mentioned by some travellers. Still, as Herodotus speaks of a *little* water, and both he and Homer speak of this as *trickling*, we ought to be content. After climbing down to the black pool at the foot of the last rock over which the water poured, we took time to let the whole setting of the Styx make its impression, which it could not fail to do. It is the setting rather than the fall which has always made the impression. Where Aroania is broken off on the east end so abruptly that one can only think of it as cut off by some gigantic cleaver, down over this front comes the Styx, not with a shoot, but hugging the rock and deflected several times along its face. Pausanias says that the precipice is the highest that he ever remembers to have seen, and its height is recorded as upward of six thousand feet. As the mountain throws out arms to the right and left of the fall, we have a place fitted to throw a potent spell over the mind on a moonlight night or at morning or evening twilight. It was here that the exiled

Cleomenes, the gifted but mad King of Sparta, made the chiefs of the Arcadians swear to support him in his attempt to secure a return to Sparta by force of arms. He doubtless took advantage of the knowledge that the Arcadians had from remote times regarded this awful place as imparting an especial sanctity to oaths, and that here particularly the warrior's oath (*sacramentum*) was taken.

It is no wonder that the lively imagination of the Greek transferred the earthly Styx to Hades, and represented the most awful and binding oath of the gods, by which they pledged their immortality, as that one which they swore by this hated and deadly water.

There is now, as there was in ancient times, a tradition that it is dangerous to drink of this water; but so great was our heat and thirst that, regardless of consequences, we drank deep at the Stygian pool. On returning home, after an interval of several days, I was caught by a lurking fever and general derangement of the system, which it required several days to throw off. I am not going to decide whether this is an example of the slowness and sureness of the gods in punishing impiety, whether I carried off a little malaria from an intervening visit at Stymphalus, or whether it was simply the result of drinking too much cold water not merely from the Styx, but from many others of the countless springs about Aroania.

Aroania, from which the Styx falls, although 7,725 feet high, is less generally known than its great neighbors east and west. When I first went to Greece I had forgotten that there was such a mountain. But it is much higher than Erymanthos, and affords a better view than Kyllene, which is about seventy feet higher. Pausanias, who was no mountain climber, ascended Aroania. Perhaps he was possessed by the idea of doing justice to everything connected with so holy a place. Following in his footsteps, we walked up to a shepherd's enclosure, at an altitude of 5,000 feet, accompanied by the owner of the flocks, who was also later our guide to the Styx. Here we spent the night in the open air, near a fire, wrapped in rugs. At half-past two we set out by the light of an old moon and reached the summit at half-past four. For two hours clouds swept past us with fierce velocity, and it was bitter cold as well as wet. It began to appear as if the same misfortune was upon us as befell us a month before, when we had climbed Parnassus to be lost in a cloud whose lifting gave us only here and there a glimpse of the world below. But now at last we did get the whole broad view from Thessaly to Taygetos. The grandest feature of all was Parnassus and the still higher mountains of Ætolia; but the most interesting and instructive feature was Peloponnesus, stretched out before us like a raised map. We could study its chains and ganglia of mountains.

Two days later we were at Lake Stymphalus. We hastened to bathe in it. Had we plunged in we should probably have achieved distinction as the first bathers in that lake; but the sight of a half a dozen blood-suckers at our feet held us back, and, bathing *from* the lake rather than in it, we came away not much cleaner for the operation. But we secured a practical insight into the nature of this lake, which is like several larger and smaller lakes in Northeastern Arcadia. Strictly speaking, it is no lake at all, but a mud-pond. Probably in no place is the water more than four or five feet deep, and had we dived from any part of the shore our heads would still be sticking in the mud.

In a normal condition of things there should be here neither lake nor mud-pond, but only a plain with a river running through it, and disappearing in a hole at the foot of the mountain at the southern end. Mountains are so thickly strewn in Arcadia that streams cannot get around them, and so have to go through them. In this case the water was supposed to find its way out under the mountains to a point somewhat south of Argos, where it rushes out of the mountain side as a pure and full river, under the name of Erasinos. But such a hole, called a *katabothra*, was always likely to get clogged, and, as a stoppage might occur at a distance from the mouth, it might be very difficult to clear it out. In spite of great care this katabothra was, doubtless, sometimes stopped in ancient times. The horrible Stymphalian birds which Heracles killed typify, it is supposed, the pestilence which arose from such a stoppage. Such gigantic labors as forcing open the katabothra are quite in keeping with the character of Heracles's other labors, which included the purging of the stables of Augeas and the draining of the marsh of Lerna, typified by the killing of the Lernæan hydra. That birds should here be chosen to represent the evil seems an apt touch of local coloring; for several times in our stay around this lake the air was shaken by a rustling of wings, and flocks of birds that looked like wild ducks settled down into the water or flew up from it.

As a proof that the water of the lake in antiquity was not up to its present level, we saw near the water's edge deep wheel ruts in the rock, which would now be deeply covered by the water in the spring (for besides the irregular variation, dependent on the more or less perfect working of the katabothra, there must always have been the regular variations, dependent on winter rains and summer drouth). Furthermore, standing on the imposing walls of the acropolis of Stymphalus, on a hill which projects from a mountain out into the marsh on its western side, one sees foundations of temples and other buildings of the lower town, hardly clear from water at the driest season of the year. Archæological excavations here would probably be particularly rewarding; but are absolutely impossible until the modern arrangements for draining the lake, begun some years ago, are carried to a higher stage of perfection than they have reached at present.

Of course there is no better drinking-water in Greece than that which flows into Lake Stymphalus. It flows from the mountains round about. Kyllene contributes a large share. It is only when it lies in the basin and stagnates there that it becomes polluted. In Hadrian's reign an aqueduct carried from this source a copious supply of water to populous Corinth, furnishing both drinking-water about as good as that of Pirene and the great amount required in the numerous baths.

Now that Athens is rapidly growing, its authorities are at their wits' ends to find a proper supply of water for the pressing needs of so large a city. All sorts of temporary expedients have been resorted to to increase the regular supply from Pentelicus. But none of them are adequate; and the minds of the far-seeing ones contemplate the necessity of bringing water from Stymphalus. Certainly if Athens is to grow at its present rate, and become a city with a population of two hundred thousand or more, something as radical as this must be adopted.

The operations of Lake Pheneus are really more interesting and important than those of Lake Stymphalus, owing to its greater size. It has been, as is seen by the marks on the surrounding rocks, at one time some one hundred feet higher than in 1895, when it was a modest lake of about three miles in diameter. In antiquity Heracles was called in even here to make a long canal, traces of which have been noted by modern travellers, straight through the plain to the katabothra at the southern end. This canal was out of repair even in Pausanias's time, and the river had reverted to its original tortuous bed. Here also the stoppage of the katabothra has been fruitful of mischief. In ancient times the strong city of Pheneos was forced to surrender by a general who stopped the katabothra, imitating the tactics by which Agesipolis took Mantineia. Once also in modern times a natural stoppage caused a general desertion of the plain, and the water gradually rose until it began to seem as if it would ultimately flow over the mountain-pass to the south, and discharge itself into the plain of Orchomenos, which already has its hands full with its own katabothra. But at the very time of the arrival in Greece of the young King Otto, the accumulated water forced the katabothra, and laid bare a tract of most richly fertilized land, an event which was regarded as a blessing bestowed upon the advent of the king. At the same time a great swelling of the Ladon and the Alpheios, resulting in an overflow of Olympia, proved conclusively, what the ancients appear to have known, that the water of Pheneos flowed into the Ladon. Since the Alpheios proper, the southern fork of the river to which the Ladon is the still greater tributary, disappears twice before it achieves an uninterrupted course, it is little wonder that the fancy of the Greek could picture it as reappearing, even after a course under the sea, at the fountain of Arethusa in Syracuse.

At the time of our visit Lake Pheneos was most impressive. Five hundred feet higher than Lake Stymphalus, it was surrounded by grander mountains, the steep slopes of which were thickly wooded on their lower parts. It had as fine a setting as a lake could have. When I was approaching it five years later from the south, I kept saying to my companions, "Now I will show you one of the finest sights in Greece." But as we advanced and more and more of the plain came into view, I began to wonder what had become of the lake. It soon transpired that it had repeated its old trick and slipped away again, leaving some fertile territory, but a larger area of sand; and, what seemed sadder than all else, converting a beautiful bit of scenery into a dry valley, not altogether unlovely it must be confessed. I was, however, much chagrined to be cheated out of my function as showman. Thus it will ever be with these lakes. When the water rises so high as to have weight enough to force out the obstruction which first produced the lake, the lake seeks the sea; and the process of stopping and opening will be repeated to the end of time.

In that part of Arcadia traversed by us there are no hotels and no carriage-roads. Most of the nights we slept on rugs spread on the floor of very plain houses. One night only did we have beds, in a so-called inn at Kalavryta, our farthest point to the north. These beds—bad success to them!—reminded us of the ancient conundrum, "When is a bed not a bed?" They kept the promise to the ear and broke it to the heart. We were more contented with the frank statement of the demarch (mayor, if one may call him so) of a little village, in whose house we spent our first night out: "You are very welcome to my house, but you will have bugs." The prophecy was amply fulfilled before morning. In no night of the whole journey were we spared this affliction. But the exaltation of spirit in such a country is great enough to make one speedily forget the annoyance to the flesh. Of course, a good deal of this annoyance might have been avoided by taking along our own beds, which would have involved only the paying for an extra horse. This plan I have subsequently followed.

There was a sameness in our meals. So soon as we arrived at our night's lodging we ordered four chickens, two for dinner and two to carry along the next day in our saddle-bags for luncheon. This with bread and unlimited grapes, without money and without price, provided us with two meals a day, and in Greece one never thinks of taking anything more in the early morning than a little coffee with bread. The grape season is the favorable time to travel in Greece. Grapes are even more than bread the staff of life; they assuage thirst as well as serve for food.

Our route was a long circuit which brought us back to Argos again through Mantineia, Orchomenos, Kleitor, Kalavryta, Megaspeleon, Styx, Pheneos, Stymphalus, Phlius, Nemea. It may be interesting to add that the whole outlay was less than ten dollars apiece, of which more than half went to the payment for horses. It is difficult to procure anywhere so much pleasure at so little expense. How different is this from the experience of the man who complained that he had spent years in wandering about Europe paying a dollar for every fifty cents' worth of pleasure!

AN UNUSUAL APPROACH TO EPIDAUROS

Perhaps the best way to study thoroughly a country, as well as to enjoy it, is to do what we do at home, namely, to wander over it at leisure, letting impressions settle in on us without making efforts to gather information. Unfortunately, we seldom have time to do this in a foreign country. I count it, therefore, as a privilege that during two successive summers a residence, once on the island of Kalauria, now called Poros, and once on the mainland opposite to it, in the territory of Troezen, furnished me an opportunity to become acquainted in this delightful way with a most interesting part of Greece. Not only did I pay frequent visits to the temple on the island, where Demosthenes committed suicide—a temple at that time being excavated by Swedish archæologists, but I also made several excursions to Troezen, Methana, and Ægina, and once, breaking through the high mountain which opposite Poros approaches the sea, I worked my way over it across the eastern prong of plane-tree-leaf-shaped Peloponnesus to the old Dryopian town of Hermione, which, in its beautiful situation at the innermost recess of a deep bay, rivals Troezen.

For several weeks during one of these summers Mr. Kabbadias, the Greek Ephor-General of Antiquities, was our next neighbor; and subsequently, when he was excavating at Epidauros, where he worked for five years after his brilliant success on the Athenian acropolis, an invitation from him was the occasion of my making a still longer excursion. My companion was a Greek neighbor. As it was summer, we made an early start, sailing along two hours to the harbor of Troezen, where we took horses which had preceded us. At five o'clock we were in the saddle. For an hour or more we skirted the shore as far as the nature of the land (if we may call bare rocks land) would allow it, passing in the rear of Methana, that jagged *sierra* which from Athens forms an impressive background for Ægina, and is itself projected against the higher mountains of the mainland. Then coming to a point where these mountains fall sheer into the sea some fifteen hundred feet, we were obliged to turn inland. The path, foreseeing the jumping-off place, took the turn betimes by climbing up with many a zigzag a face of the mountain which was not quite perpendicular. After a long pull we passed on our right a village called Lower Phanari, which looked so much like an eyrie that one might think "Lower" was added in jest. But when with still more toil we reached another village called Upper Phanari, and looked down upon the other, we recognized the seriousness of the distinction. There it lay, with its fifty-one houses, so far below us that it seemed almost level with the sea.

Why anybody should ever choose to live so high up on the rocks as Upper Phanari was not at first apparent. But after a halt here for luncheon (brought with us, of course, for no traveller counts on living on such a region), and after two hours of refreshing sleep on wooden benches, we moved downward and inland, and in a quarter of an hour came upon one of those little plains which supported so many villages in ancient Greece. In this case an ancient village, the name of which we may never know, and which occupied the site of Upper Phanari, where it has left substantial traces of itself in the shape of walls, must have got a scanty support from this little plain. Both ancients and moderns, rather than live in the plain, preferred to live on the rocks above, although it entailed carrying the produce and drinking water a mile, that they might live in sight of the beloved sea. Our downward turn was soon exchanged for another upward one, our course being all the time northward and parallel to the shore. Once a great gap in the range separating us from the sea revealed not only the sea, but the whole of Methana, which, with all its height, was so low that we looked over its peaks down into the sea. About four o'clock, refusing a turn into a broad mountain valley to the left, we turned sharply to the right and broke through the mountains by a narrow gorge, and were again on the outside with the whole Saronic Gulf before us. It was such a display of beauty that one shrinks from enumerating its details. What immediately arrested our attention was that which lay at our feet. Here the mountains receded a little, giving place to a paradise of vines and trees, which made a marked contrast to the brown mountains on the one hand, and the blue sea on the other. The boundary lines of each color were very sharp. A large opening, very little of which we could see, ran back into the mountain to the left of the plain. Through this opening a stream came down, flowing even in the summer, a rare thing in Eastern Greece.

This plain contained the ancient town of Epidauros, and three hours' distant, up through the opening in the mountains, lay the sanctuary of Æsculapius, called to-day the Hieron or Holy Place, which gave the town its importance. One travelling from Athens to Nauplia by sea is attracted by this single opening on the whole eastern shore of Argolis. But much as one would like to turn in here and explore the great opening, and go this way up to the "holy place," the steamers take him along past it, unless he perchance gets off at Ægina, and trusts himself to a sail-boat to take him across. Travellers generally have to follow the beaten track; and I had visited the Hieron four times by the longer route from Nauplia before it befell me to approach it by this road, which was trodden by the greater part of the tens of thousands who came to seek salvation from Æsculapius.

We now wound our way down the mountain side, entering the village of Epidauros at sunset, along with the troops of vintagers, from whose crates we took grapes to our hearts' content. As for any payment, nobody thought of that. Now I got an interesting lesson in Greek hospitality. My companion had brought a letter of introduction to a man in this village whom we met coming in from his vineyard. He said that he was very busy disposing of his grapes, and could hardly be at his house at all that night. But he called one of his workmen and told him to take us to his house and see that we had the best room in it. We did not see him again until the next morning, when we met him already among his vines at four o'clock, three miles up the valley on the road to the Hieron. The pressure of New England haymaking is nothing compared with that of the vintage season in Greece.

Nothing could exceed the cordiality of our host in these two encounters by evening and morning twilight. His hospitality was as hearty as it was a matter of course. Angels could have done no more. It was, in the Homeric phrase, δόσις ὀλίγη τε φίλη τε. His off-hand hospitality was to us a perfect godsend. We were lodged in the best house in the village, and made as free and easy as if we had been in an inn. Without him we should have come off short. The village contained only about thirty houses, and most of these very uninviting. In fact, a stranger would hardly seek shelter in any of them except under stress of weather. There is hardly a more neglected corner in Greece than this once important place, the mother city of Ægina, which lies in plain sight confronting it, two hours' sail across the bay. Not only does no steamer put in here, but there was not even a sail-boat in the harbor while we were there. We were told that no sail-boat was owned by anybody in the village, an unheard-of thing on a Greek coast. To send a telegram or to get a physician one must send to Piada, called also New Epidauros, an hour and a half distant. A mail comes twice a week on horseback from Nauplia, all the way across the peninsula.

In this neglected but most picturesque corner remain the walls of a stately acropolis on a rocky peninsula with a harbor on each side of it, and other remains of a great city protruding from the rich soil where this peninsula joins the mainland.

But while the city has perished, the Hieron has, in a certain sense, come to life again. Here an area has been laid bare much larger than that excavated by the Germans at Olympia. The theatre, the best preserved of all Greek theatres, was never entirely covered up, and was early and easily cleared. The project of having a grand presentation of ancient dramas here has often been broached but never carried out, on account of the difficulty of transporting and feeding the spectators necessary to the success of the project, to say nothing of lodging them. The acoustic properties of this theatre are well known. One standing in front of the stage makes himself heard without effort by one sitting in the top row of seats.

The finest building in the precinct was the so-called Tholos, a round building as highly ornamented as the Erechtheum at Athens, and boasting Polycleitus as its architect. The temple of Æsculapius was almost equally brilliant, but these two buildings do not exist except to the archæologist. We have inscriptions giving most elaborate accounts of the construction of each of them; but of each building nothing remains except their foundations and broken fragments of their brilliant adornment. Were it not for giving this description of a journey the appearance of a guide-book, I might speak of the Herculean labors of Mr. Kabbadias in excavating the Stadion, and the little pleasure that the sight of it affords the layman.

THEATRE AT EPIDAUROS

The great interest of the excavation really centres in the inscriptions discovered. Mr. Kabbadias looked up from his arduous work, the hot afternoon of our arrival, upon a much-defaced inscription, and said with an enthusiasm which means much in a quiet man: "I tell you no man has a right to think that he understands Greek life if he has not read these inscriptions of Epidauros." These inscriptions, at any rate, kept him from sleeping during the afternoon hours of summer days when nearly all Greeks sleep, even if they do not sleep nights.

Among this material there is, perhaps, nothing more interesting than two long inscriptions, each containing records of twenty or more cases of miraculous cures wrought on sick people who came here and went to sleep in a long porch, remains of which survive. The cures are mostly wrought in dreams. Here is a sample (I quote from the stone):

"Case of a man with a cancer in his stomach. He went to sleep and had a vision. The god seemed to him to command his attendants to seize him and hold him that he might cut open his stomach. He himself seemed to be trying to run away; but the attendants caught him and bound him, while Æsculapius opened his stomach, cut out the cancer, sewed up the incision, and released him from his bonds. And after this he went away healed; and the floor of the apartment was covered with blood."

The following case ascribes to the god the power to work cures upon an absent person:

"Case of Arata of Sparta having dropsy. Her mother, leaving her in Sparta, slept and had a vision. It seemed to her that the god cut off her daughter's head and hung up the body with the neck downward, and when a great quantity of water had run out, took the body down again and replaced the head upon the neck. After she had seen the vision she returned to Sparta, and found her daughter restored to health, having seen the same vision."

As if to put the seal of verification upon these cases, two inscriptions tell of doubters who were convinced of the god's power to heal, against their will. One records the case of a man with all the fingers of one hand paralyzed except one, who, seeing these tablets in the sacred precinct recording the miraculous cures, laughed and doubted:

"Now this man, in his sleep, seemed to see the god seize hold of his hand and straighten out his fingers, and when the man, in doubt, kept opening and shutting his fingers to see whether it were really true, the god seemed to ask him if he *now* doubted the truth of the inscriptions. When the man replied that he was convinced, the god said to him: 'Because you did not at once believe things that were in no wise incredible I give you the name of "The Doubter."'"

This was the only vengeance inflicted by the mild god upon this "doubting Thomas"; for "when day dawned he went away healed."

Some think that this great healing establishment had two strings to its bow, and that alongside of the miraculous cures which drew the crowd there was a treatment which approached in some degree the regular practice of medicine. At any rate it is clear that water played a great rôle here, not only from the inscriptions, but also from the fact that the precinct is honeycombed with water-pipes. Sunlight and good air were also doubtless operative. The Hieron lies in a bowl, high up, it is true, but finely protected from the winds, especially the north wind and east wind. It possesses the qualities of a good winter resort. In summer it is now somewhat hot, but the air is certainly not so sultry as in the lower lying parts of Argolis. As the precinct is spoken of in ancient times as a "grove," there must then have been abundant shade all about. Numerous porches also, with various exposures, gave an option between sun and shade. We should not go far astray in speaking of the Hieron as an ancient Carlsbad as well as an ancient Lourdes. But in its material equipment it was greatly superior to both; for from very early times down through the days of the Antonines one noble building after another was reared here under the supervision of the best architects.

When the cool of the day had come on we strolled over the sacred precinct, and then with Mr. Kabbadias and his family took dinner at a table set in the open air just behind the stage building. Close by us was the fine *cavea* of the theatre, resplendent with the light of a summer full-moon. It is easily understood that such a visit is more impressive than the usual one from Nauplia, in which most of the day is taken up in coming and going and one has but about three hours to see the place and take a hurried luncheon.

Rising the next morning at two o'clock from our mattresses on the floor beside the statues in the museum, we struck into a more Alpine road even than that by which we had come, into the roughest part of Argolis. At eight o'clock we passed the water-shed between the Argolic and the Saronic gulfs, from which both are plainly visible, and here, high up between Ortholithi and the Didyma, we took our well-earned breakfast beside a spring. At noon we were at the ruins of Troezen, and so almost home.

MESSENE AND SANDY PYLOS

In passing from Olympia to Sparta by sea in 1891 I had put into the harbor of Pylos at sunset; and had not fellow-travellers urged me on I could not have resisted the powerful charm of the place. A hurried visit to Ithome the next day afforded some compensation, and Sparta, approached by the magnificent Langadha Pass through Taygetos, made me forget my loss entirely. But for years that sunset and nightfall lingered in my memory, accompanied by the hope of letting the impression of Pylos deepen upon me by a second visit. Ten years and a half later I found myself again in Messenia, with the full intention of filling up the gap in my acquaintance with that corner of Greece; but it was December, and a heavy rain set in and drove our party back to Athens by rail.

In January of the present year six of us took the train at Athens for Kalamata, the modern capital of Messenia. It was immediately after a heavy fall of snow; and we hoped at least to revel in the sight of Arcadia presenting a Swiss aspect, but indulged also the larger hope of studying carefully Messene, and especially Pylos. Neither hope failed us; Arcadia was magnificent in its winter dress. In Tripolitza, which is over two thousand feet high, the snow lay several inches thick, and the train threaded its way among mountains carrying heavy masses of it. The journey paid for itself.

But a series of April days followed. The first of them we spent in the "blessed plain" adjacent to Kalamata, which far surpasses all the rest of Greece in exuberant fertility. Semi-tropical vegetation, heavily loaded orange-trees, vineyards hidden by enormous hedges of cactus, with a full flowing river, make one huge garden. But the setting is more magnificent than the jewel itself. A deep bay comes running up on the south; Taygetos towers to the east, and less magnificent mountains to the north. Only on the west is the plain bordered by a low range which looks rather tame, but which later gave us work enough to get across it on our way to Pylos. The goal of our first day's journey lay about fifteen miles to the north, where, between two considerable peaks on the west side of the "blessed valley," lay the Messene of the fourth century before Christ, founded by Epaminondas.

Tardy restitution given to a long-suffering people; late righting of an ancient wrong! Let us not, however, think of Epaminondas as acting out of pure benevolence. He was studying the best means of putting a check upon the power of Sparta. For some two centuries and a half Sparta's heel had rested heavily on this people, its nearest kin, who were by no means weaklings, if we can put any trust in the tales of the first and second Messenian wars. Twice in those fierce struggles the balance was held nearly even for almost a generation, when it tipped in favor of Sparta; and the Messenian state sank in blood and slavery. At last the fulness of time had come, and with it Sparta's doom. The Delphic oracle given to Aristodemos centuries before was fulfilled: "Do as fate directs, but ruin falls on some before others."

The exiles were called back from far and near. So tenacious had they been of their dialect that they became a people in the most natural way in the world. That they loved their land is no wonder. The new city made by Epaminondas was laid out at the foot of Mount Ithome, perhaps on the site of an older city. At any rate, Ithome was the fortress in which Aristodemos made the last stand against Sparta in the first war. In the small Greek world the sensation caused by the reappearance of the Messenian state may be compared to that which would be felt in Europe to-day if Poland should again take her place among the nations.

So great had been the vicissitudes of the Messenian people that Pausanias for once drops his rôle of periegete to become the historian of a gallant race that succumbed to force and fate. But what history! Besides quoting the poet Tyrtæus he gives as his principal sources of information one prose historian and one poetical historian. The prose writer, Myron of Priene, he thinks "reveals an indifference to truth." One might think, then, that Pausanias was intent on sifting out the pure grain and throwing away the chaff. But the following is a fair sample of the kind of history that he serves up for us.

The first Messenian war had lasted twenty years, with varying success and failure; but at that point the Delphic oracle told the Messenians that the party which first dedicated a hundred tripods in the sanctuary of Ithomian Zeus would surely win. The Messenians were elated, thinking that surely nobody could do this but themselves, since they held that sanctuary; but to make sure of it, since bronze was scarce, they at once set about making the tripods of wood. But the oracle leaked out in Sparta; and "an insignificant fellow, but with brains," made a hundred little clay tripods, and, slinging them over his shoulder in a bag, went up to Ithome as a hunter, escaping notice by his "mere insignificance"; and after dark crept into the sanctuary and set up his little tripods around the altar of Zeus. When the Messenians saw them in the morning they had not a doubt that all was lost. The king, Aristodemos, incontinently committed suicide. But others fought on hopelessly to the bitter end, losing all their generals and men of prominence. The second war, of little less duration, came to an end with another Delphic oracle. The great fortress Eira on the northern border had been stoutly defended for years, when the Pythian priestess said: "When a he-goat drinks Neda's eddying water I will save Messene no longer, for destruction is near."

For a time there was great hustling to keep the he-goats away from the River Neda. But one day a seer noticed a wild fig-tree, which in Messenian parlance was called *tragos*, a he-goat, growing crooked, and bending over the Neda so as to brush the water with the tips of its leaves. He showed this to the general, Aristomenes, who agreed with him that all was lost; but instead of committing suicide like the leader in the former war, he fought on like a real hero, and even after the cause was lost became a terror to the Spartans on their own side of Taygetos. One wonders whether a people ever really believed that the issue of great wars turned on such portents. Such yarns may have been spun several centuries after the events, by the more or less mendacious historians, to whom Pausanias, in his character of historian, refers as his sources from which he drew his pure history of Messenia.

But however flimsy the history of those past centuries, the walls of the new city are solid reality. Pausanias records that "the first day was devoted to prayer and sacrifice; but on the following days they proceeded to rear the circuit wall, and to build houses and sanctuaries within." Why did he not say "the following *years*"? These walls are so extensive, as well as so massive, that one wonders whether they could have been built in less than five years. But there was every reason that the wall should be built at once, to secure the new city against the attacks of Sparta; and we have so many cases of rapid wall-building on the part of the Greeks that we can believe almost any feat ascribed to them in this line. Pausanias recognizes these walls as something extraordinary, saying: "I have not seen the walls of Babylon, nor the Memnonian walls at Susa in Persia, nor have I heard of them from persons who have seen them; but Ambrosos in Phokis, Byzantium, and Rhodes are fortified in the best style; and yet the walls of Messene are stronger than theirs." A great deal of this circuit wall, over five miles in extent, has now disappeared; but, on the north side the Arcadian gate, with adjacent towers and lines of wall, not only justifies Pausanias's admiration, but makes the visitor of to-day stand long in mute astonishment. The walls of Tiryns are of more gigantic blocks; but they made simply an enclosure of a palace.

The view from the top of Ithome, which towers above the city, is superb; but Pausanias must have thought it much higher than it really is when he said, "There is no higher mountain in the Peloponnesus." Taygetos, which stared him in the face, is more than five thousand feet higher; so are Kyllene and Aroania. But it is, with the possible exception of Vlocho, the acropolis of the Thestiæi, in Ætolia, the highest acropolis in Greece, measured, not from the sea level, but from the plain at its foot.

Pylos is about thirty miles distant from Kalamata, across the western prong of the Peloponnesus. Our maps led us to think that there was a fair road across. But more than fifty persons assured us that it was impossible for bicycles. We were convinced, however, that we knew better than they what one could accomplish with bicycles, knowing from experience that a bridle-path is often better than a poor carriage-road. We took the train, however, as far as Nisi (officially styled Messene, though ten miles distant from the

Messene of classical times), thus cutting off about seven miles of our journey. In the face of loud and universal dissuasion we struck out for Pylos, and in two hours we had cut off seven miles more of the road, having dismounted perhaps fifty times when it was either too muddy or too sandy, or when the path became six inches wide and two feet deep. An occasional orange plucked from an overhanging bough was a consolation for hard work. We had not yet drawn far away from the sea, and had passed, by fairly good bridges, six rivers. But now we came to a river with no bridge. While we were hesitating, a man came out of a hut near by and offered to carry us across, wheels and all, for a drachma apiece. While he was rapidly lowering his price we had got over, boy fashion, each for himself, with the added pleasure of a very cold foot-bath.

Directly after this the road took a turn up a mountain side, over rough rock strata set on edge. For the middle third of the journey the worst that had been said was short of the horrible truth. We toiled up and down over the path of jagged stones, carrying our wheels and bags. Not until two hours before sunset did we get our first glimpse of the western sea; and darkness fell upon us before we reached the carriage-road running along the shore northward from Pylos. We even struck a bog in the dark; but by keeping straight on we staggered out upon the firm road at last, probably with something of the feeling which Ulysses had when he tumbled ashore at Scheria after his long swim. Three hours later we were sleeping on beds by no means so soft as the bog from which we had been delivered.

BAY OF NAVARINO, WITH OLD PYLOS TO THE RIGHT AND SPHAKTERIA TO THE LEFT

The Pylos, where we passed the night, is a comparatively new town, having grown up around a fort built by the Franks in the thirteenth century on the south side of a great bay. Venetians occupied it later. It received, also, the name of Navarino from some merchants of Navarre, who settled there in the fifteenth century. This new Pylos, beautifully situated, looks out upon a scene so lovely that words fail to describe it; and in this spot history has been made.

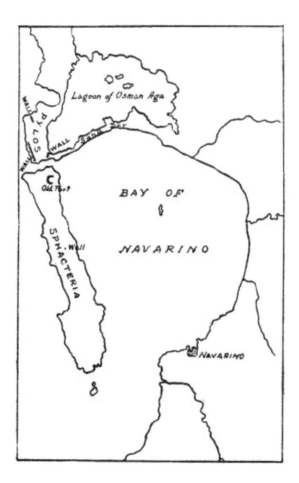

The Bay of Navarino, about three miles long from north to south, and about two miles broad, is a large natural harbor, shut off from the sea by what was in prehistoric ages a long, continuous cliff, but which in historic times had already been broken open in three places. The opening farthest north had ages ago already been silted up with sand; and the next one is in a fair way to become so before long. The northern end of the bay has also been a good deal silted up by streams flowing into it; and a long sand-bar has at last entirely shut it off from the rest, making of it a lake.

The particular feature which imparts picturesqueness to the bay is the already mentioned cliff, which rises almost perpendicularly in the greater part of its extent to a height varying from one hundred to three hundred feet, or even more. The face of these cliffs is in places very red, and when struck by the morning sun they are gorgeously colored.

In the fifth century before Christ the southern section of the hill was called Sphacteria, and was, of course, an island; the section next it on the north, which would have been an island had not the opening to the north of it been silted up, was called Pylos; after that follows a low promontory well joined to the mainland. There can be little doubt that the name Pylos is a survival of Homeric times, and that here we must look for the home of Nestor. It has become a fashion in the past few years to look for the Homeric Pylos farther north, partly to furnish a better road for Telemachos's chariot ride from Pylos to Sparta, and partly because no Mycenæan remains have been found here. But it is about as easy to take Telemachos straight over Taygetos as it is to find any more convenient road farther north. Pheræ, where the two days' journey was divided by a night's rest, has been reasonably well identified with some ancient walls on the slope of Taygetos above Kalamata; and if the journey was undertaken from our Pylos it would be about evenly divided there.

Furthermore, in the great cave on the north end of Pylos, which is probably the cave where, according to legend, the baby Hermes hid the oxen of Apollo which he had stolen, there were found in 1896 vase fragments of Mycenæan and even of pre-Mycenæan times. Who knows how soon serious excavations may bring to light Mycenæan walls under the great Venetian fortress? Such a harbor as this could hardly have failed to be known and occupied in the earliest times; and surely there is sand enough here to justify Homer's standing epithet of "Sandy Pylos."

But if the Homeric glory should be stolen away, this bay would yet be remembered as the scene of that most picturesque of naval battles in which the allied fleet, sailing in through the broad southern entrance one afternoon in 1827, annihilated in two hours the Ottoman fleet, and brought about the independence of Greece. Some of the wrecks from this battle are still to be seen on shore and beneath the water.

But, after all, it is an episode in the Peloponnesian war that has given this region its chief renown. This episode has been described in the luminous narrative of Thucydides; and the land and the book so exactly coincide that we can trace every movement of the Athenians and Spartans in that struggle of more than two months' duration. In one respect only is Thucydides's topography wide of the mark, for that he makes Sphacteria a mile too short is not important; he says that the southern entrance is broad enough for eight ships to sail in abreast, whereas it is approximately a mile wide. The whole Athenian fleet of fifty ships could easily sail in in line. Arnold of Rugby felt this difficulty so strongly that in his edition of Thucydides he advanced the view that Pylos was Sphacteria, supposing that the third opening at the time of Thucydides had not been silted up. He then sought Pylos in the northern promontory of the mainland. This, however, was jumping out of the frying-pan into the fire; for if one makes the middle mass Sphacteria the large island to the south, generally taken to be Sphacteria, is utterly ignored. There is no doubt that Thucydides in this one point departed from his principle of always getting information from eye-witnesses. Some have thought he got this broad opening confounded with a narrower one, which at that time, before the sand-bar reached clear up to Pylos, as it now does, led into the northern part of the bay, a sort of lagoon, affording a secure harbor, in which the Spartan fleet awaited attack, supported, morally at least, by the proximity of their land forces. In every other point the narrative fits the minutest *nuances* of hill and shore.

Most unexpectedly the seat of war was transferred to this quarter. In the spring of 425 B.C. an Athenian fleet was sailing past Pylos bound for Sicily, on which Athens even then had her eye, with instructions to attend first to the Spartan fleet that was hovering off Kerkyra, trying to bring the island over to the Peloponnesian alliance by the aid of their partisans then in exile near at hand. Accompanying the fleet was Demosthenes, the man of deeds, whose path through this war is marked with brightness. Ever capable and adequate to every emergency, he was at last destroyed, and Athens with him, by the incompetency of Nikias. In the previous year he had gained in Akarnania the greatest Athenian victory of the war, cutting off all the able-bodied men of Ambrakia and luring Sparta into a discreditable abandonment of her allies. In the full enjoyment of the public confidence he accompanied the fleet, with indefinite powers to use it in any way that seemed to be for the good of Athens.

When they were off Pylos he saw there, in that deserted region, a chance to strike a deadly blow at Sparta. He proposed to fortify Pylos, and establish there Messenians, who, knowing the land and loving it, would be a thorn in the side of Sparta. But the Admirals, Eurymedon and Sophokles, felt that the chief function of the fleet was to save Kerkyra, inasmuch as Athens had entered into the war depending upon the help that this great naval power could give. They refused to stop, telling Demosthenes that there were headlands enough on the shores of Peloponnesus as good as this, if he really wanted to throw away the money of Athens in fortifying them. He had no power of coercion; but he tried every form of persuasion. The men agreed with the Admirals; but he turned to the captains; and when they also refused to help him out he had to abandon his plan and move on with the rest. The relation of Demosthenes to the fleet seems droll. But by his strong personality, aided by luck, he accomplished all, and perhaps more than all, that he had hoped for.

The fleet had hardly put out to sea when, luckily for him, a storm came on, and they were all driven back into the bay for shelter. The storm continued for several days, and after awhile the men by a common impulse began to fortify Pylos. It was a regular lark. They had brought along no tools to cut stones; so they took stones which lay ready at hand and piled them up just as they happened to fit. They used their backs as hods to carry mud, clasping their hands low down behind them and letting their companions load them up. Two short stretches of wall at the north and south ends made Pylos secure from attack on the land side. Another longer one, but not so high, on the sea front at the southwest angle was a sort of lure to invite attack by sea. In front of the wall was the only level space on Pylos; but before one could reach it by sea he must run his ship in close to a belt of jagged rocks, and get across them as best he could. Demosthenes, who was the director of all this jolly activity, frankly told his men that he never meant to fight behind this wall, but in front of it; never allowing a man of the enemy to reach the shore.

In six days the work of fortification was completed; and the Admirals went on, leaving Demosthenes and five of their forty ships to carry out his plan. By good luck his men, who were marines and not very well equipped for land fighting, were immediately re-enforced by a Messenian pirate boat, with a lot of wicker shields on board, and, to crown all, forty heavy armed soldiers (hoplites).

Before a blow was struck this simple lodgment of Demosthenes brought about two great results. The Spartan fleet hastened back to the spot, slipping past the Athenian fleet; and the Spartan army, which had made the annual invasion of Attica, came hastily back to Sparta after only fifteen days of occupation. The fleet occupied the bay, and the land army butted its head in vain against the walls on that side. Then came the attempt which Demosthenes had expected. They tried to land in front of his sea-wall. But as the handful of men in possession held their ground not a Spartan reached the shore, though the gallant Brasidas, who here appears as the simple commander of a trireme, tried it with a daring that nearly cost him his life. For nearly two days this attack continued. It failed as signally as the land attack. The Spartans were at their wits' ends. They had sent to Asine, a day's journey distant, for big timbers to make battering-rams and break down the walls toward the mainland. They also landed a force on the island, Sphacteria, to overawe by their proximity the Athenians across the narrow channel, and to prevent any future lodgment of the Athenians on Sphacteria also.

When the Spartan fleet had first appeared Demosthenes had sent two of his five triremes to advise the Athenian Admirals that the plot was thickening; and the Athenian fleet, strengthened to fifty sail, appeared off the entrances of the bay; but seeing both entrances defended by the Spartan fleet and the shore crowded with Spartan soldiers, it put about, and, going back to an island a few miles to the north, passed the night there. This was probably a ruse to throw the Spartans off their guard; for the next day the Athenians reappeared, and with no hesitation drove in at both entrances upon the Spartans, who were evidently not thoroughly prepared. After a long and fierce struggle the victory of the Athenians was decisive. They erected a trophy, gave up the Spartan dead, took possession of the wrecks and many of the sound vessels of the enemy, and sailed at will around the bay and the entrances. The main army of the Spartans lay close at hand; but all their hope of getting materials for battering down Demosthenes's landward walls, or of starving out his little band, was cut off.

The whole situation was changed at a single blow. The centre of interest shifts to the island, Sphacteria, where the Spartans were now imprisoned. The Athenians thought them sure game, and patrolled the island to cut off escape. The situation was so serious that the highest magistrates of Sparta appeared on the scene, and, after surveying the situation, decided that the only thing to do was to propose a truce. And a truce was immediately agreed upon, all the Spartan ships being given over to the Athenians as a pledge until Spartan envoys could be taken to Athens on an Athenian trireme and secure a permanent treaty of peace.

The envoys went and begged for peace, but the party in power at Athens made too great demands, and the envoys returned *re infecta*. The Athenians, claiming some slight infraction of the treaty, refused to deliver over the ships.

All interest was now centred on the fate of the Spartans shut up on Sphacteria. Instead of laying down their arms they waited for the Athenians to "come and take them." The starving process failed, because daring Spartans on shore were found who risked their lives to carry in provisions. Helots, especially, ran every risk, securing freedom as the price of success. The Athenians themselves suffered terribly, inasmuch as they controlled only the sea, and so were forced to take their meals in cramped quarters or in imminent fear of attack by the dreaded Spartan hoplite. More painful still was the lack of good drinking water. They were obliged to scratch away the sand with their hands and drink brackish sea water. The Spartans on the island had a well which afforded much better water. When this strain had lasted nearly two months the patience of the Athenians gave out. But just at this critical time a fire was accidentally started on the island by some Athenians who were cooking their dinner there, out of sight of the Spartans. Nearly the whole island, which was uninhabited and heavily wooded, was burned over. For the first time the Athenians were able to see how few the enemy were, and to watch their movements. Demosthenes, now the soul of every movement, resolved to attack them. But in the meantime tidings of the sad plight and sufferings of the besiegers had been carried to Athens, and a stormy and somewhat amusing scene had taken place in the Athenian Assembly, in which Cleon, the leader of the majority, who had been responsible for the failure of the peace negotiations, was compelled, much against his will, to go to Pylos, as commander, "to show how easy it was to take the Spartans by force." But he arrived in the nick of time, and, by trusting everything to Demosthenes, he went back to Athens with the captives within the few days in which he had boastfully said he would do it. It was, however, well understood at Athens that the planner and executer of the deed was Demosthenes. Aristophanes, in the Knights, makes Demosthenes say: "Out at Pylos I had kneaded up a Spartan cake, and Cleon, in a most rascally manner, snatched it away and served it up." Demosthenes landed on the island a force of about fifteen thousand men, mostly light armed, who could skip about over the rocks and burnt trees, inflicting injuries on the Spartan hoplites without suffering much in return. There were only 420 Spartans, and no note is taken of their attendant light armed. If we allow seven such attendants to each of them, which is a usual proportion, we should have a total force of 3,360; but as Thucydides says nothing of light armed troops on the Spartan side, but makes it an affair of hoplites against light armed, there was probably not a large body of auxiliaries present to the Spartans; but allowing the maximum, the opposing forces were in a proportion of five to one. If, however, the light armed attendants were lacking, the proportion was about fifty to one. Never in all Spartan history did their splendid fighting machine better show its superiority than in the slow march from the well at the centre of the island to the "old fort" at the north end. Demosthenes had distributed his light armed, in detachments of several hundred each, all along the line of march. His small force of hoplites, every time it was confronted by the Spartans, fell back at once and gave place to the light armed, who, with arrows and javelins, inflicted severe losses, easily keeping out of reach of the Spartan spears. There was, in fact, no serious loss to chronicle on the Athenian side. But that the little company led by Epitidas should move steadily toward its goal during the whole of a long summer day, half stifled with ashes and smoke, oppressed by raging thirst, surrounded by yelling thousands and pelted by every kind of missile, without the slightest thought of surrender, is perhaps the most brilliant page in the annals of Sparta. However much we may be inclined to throw up our cap at every success of Athens, we must here assign the honors to the vanquished. The movement of the Spartans over that mile and a half reminds us of a lion worried by a pack of yelping hounds.

Epitidas, and after him the second in command, had been killed before the little band reached the fort, which is made in a semicircle around the west side of the peak to which the island rises on the northeast. When they got inside this the attack slackened. But the end came by a turn that one can hardly understand, even with all the explanation afforded by an exact knowledge of the lay of the land. A Messenian captain told the Athenian leaders that they were wasting time and men, but that he knew a way to approach the Spartans in the rear. His suggestion being accepted, he, with a few desperate men, scrambled up a precipice and appeared suddenly on the summit in the rear of the Spartans.

The mystery is how this could have been so unexpected by the Spartans; a single picket posted on the summit, only a few paces distant from the line that they were defending, could have seen the approach of the new enemy. How could they have failed to keep such a watch? But the sudden appearance of the Messenians is regarded as closing the fight. The Athenian commanders preferred to capture rather than kill, and so summoned the survivors to surrender. They then lowered their shields. Their commander at once asked permission to communicate with the Spartan army on the mainland. This was granted; and when the answer came back, "The Lacedemonians bid you act as you think best; but you are not to dishonor yourselves," they consulted and surrendered. Of the 420 Spartan hoplites, 120 surrendered. That a hundred Spartans had surrendered on the field of battle threw Greece into wild amazement, and broke the spell of Sparta's supposed invincibility until it was restored again by Agis on the field of Mantineia seven years later.

In modern warfare we consider it folly to throw away life after the battle is absolutely decided; and on Sphacteria we bow our heads reverently to the Spartans who, after a fight never surpassed in the world's history, dared to surrender and save their lives for the good of Sparta. When, however, we pass over to Pylos we pass to an admiration of Demosthenes, who planting himself in the midst of dangers, outwitted and outfought the enemy in superior numbers; and, by his wise plan, brought Sparta into such a position that, had Athens possessed a statesman wise enough to use it, she might have concluded an honorable peace which would have left her victor in the struggle into which Pericles led her with his eyes wide open. But Cleon let the golden opportunity pass through his fingers. The handful of heroes that were paraded so long in Athens were only a miserable residuum of the lost opportunity.

DALMATIA,
NORTHERN SECTION.

DALMATIA,
SOUTHERN SECTION.

SICILY.

A TOUR IN SICILY

It was with an appetite whetted by long waiting that I landed in Sicily on the last day of May, 1897. *Anybody* might enjoy travel in Sicily. Its scenery is magnificent. A mountainous country with a coast-line of rugged headlands, and here and there a river breaking through to the sea, opening up vistas into the interior and forming a fertile plain at its mouth; above all, snow-capped and smoking Ætna, with its nearly eleven thousand feet towering so high as to be seen from every part of the island except the valleys, form a combination attractive even to one who has left history and art out of his travelling outfit. The student of history, however, gets a keener enjoyment in this land where so much history—ancient, mediæval, and modern—has been enacted. Not only was it the apple of discord between Rome and Carthage, but, to say nothing of Sikans, Elymi, and Sikels, because their movements are wrapped in the mist of a prehistoric past, Phœnicians, Greeks, Carthaginians, Romans, Franks, Vandals, Goths, Byzantines, Saracens, Normans, Germans, French, and Spaniards successively shaped its destinies until Garibaldi at last brought it to rest in the bosom of the kingdom of Italy. But Sicily has an especial interest for the student of the history and art of ancient Greece. He who studies the country now known as Greece and neglects the greater Hellas in the west makes a great mistake. Akragas and Selinus have left more imposing ruins than Athens, Olympia, and Delphi; and Syracuse was at one time the most populous and the most powerful of all Greek cities.

It was this especial claim which drew me and my two companions, members of the American School at Athens, to Catania. We desired to become as familiar with western Hellas as we had already become with eastern Hellas. We came rather too late in the year; not that physical comfort is an element for great consideration in such a land; it is rather the psychological aspect which I have in mind. Theocritus has thrown such associations of spring over Sicily that the traveller feels that he ought to be there with "pulses thronged with the fulness of the spring," which can hardly be the case in the great heat of June. Perhaps our bicycles might seem to some out of time with Theocritus and Pindar, and we did not try to throw any glamour of poetry over them. But they were vastly convenient. We had sent forward our heavy luggage to Palermo, and they carried all that we needed for two weeks. While they were not a substitute for trains, they freed us from servile dependence on trains. If a train went our way at our time, as it did from Syracuse to Girgenti, we took it. But finding no railroad connection between Girgenti and Selinus, except such as took us across to the north side of the island and then back again to the south side, we passed the intervening space in a direct line along the southern shore, saving both time and money. When we were at Syracuse we wished to visit the river Asinaros, where the fugitive Athenian army was brought to bay and slaughtered and captured. The five o'clock train was too early. Who likes to take a morning meal at half-past four with the fear of losing a train before his eyes? Discomfort if not dyspepsia hovers over him. The alternative of a later train involved giving up the day to this excursion, and we needed that day for something else. We took a comfortable meal, and, starting at six o'clock, at a quarter past eight were on the banks of the Asinaros, and by the aid of a train were back in Syracuse at ten o'clock, ready for a good day's work.

Our beginning was inauspicious. A chapter of small accidents on the lava-paved streets of Catania kept us hovering around a shop presided over by a woman in which sewing-machines and a few other miscellaneous machines, including bicycles, were repaired. Here, in a subordinate position, was one of those mechanics who know how to do things as if by instinct, a not unworthy successor of Hephæstos, who used to do business on a grander scale hard by, with Ætna for his forge. Your real mechanic, from Tubal Cain down, is always the right man in the right place. A deft-handed New Hampshire mechanic once said to me, after putting some dislocated object to rights in less than five minutes, "I shall have to charge you ten cents for doing the job and fifteen cents for knowing how." It struck me as a good expression of the claims of the guild.

When we got off it was nearly eleven o'clock, and the flower of the day was gone; but we had vowed to see the sunrise from the theatre of Taormina the next morning; and so we sped off in the heat over roads so bad as to make us repent of all the hard things we had said of the roads of Greece. A good deal of the way lay between Ætna and the sea over lava-beds of various ages, among them the identical stream which, coming down fresh and hot, turned Himilco from proceeding straight against Dionysius and Syracuse after the destruction of Messina, and obliged him to make the circuit of the awful mountain. Shortly after noon we passed, on the highest of these lava-beds, Acireale, the most important of several Acis, all of which commemorate Acis, who here, to his grief, associated with Galatea and Polyphemus. Near by are several jagged islands pointed out by tradition as the very rocks which the latter hurled at Ulysses with such poor results. From this point on Taormina lay clear before us in the distance, high up above the sea, though but a short horizontal distance from it. When we reached Giardini, the village on the seashore which serves as a railroad station for Taormina, parched with heat and thirst, we were reminded of the verse of Euripides, "The sea washes away all human ills," and we here began a series of baths with which we encircled the island. Nemesis marked me when, in exuberance of spirit, I made the understatement, "This bath is worth a dollar," and made it cost me just that amount. Between the road and the shore was a railroad with a cactus hedge on each side of it. In passing this I hardly noticed that my wheel had lightly brushed against a cactus plant. But we had hardly begun the ascent to Taormina before my wheel was in a state of collapse.

Well, the morrow must take thought for the things of itself. Here was Taormina for us to enjoy. We had planned to spend one night only here, because there was little material for archæological study except the famous theatre, which in its present state is Roman. It was indeed refreshing to see near the upper rim of the theatre, and partly covered by its massive but cheap-looking walls of brick, the foundations of a Greek temple in four courses with its perfect joints of stone. But while Syracuse and Girgenti and Selinus were our proper fields for study, Taormina was for pleasure. From this eyrie, Ætna, which from Catania is in some degree disappointing, as is even Mont Blanc when seen from Chamonix, rises as grandly as does Mont Blanc when seen from the heights across the valley, Flégère or Brévent; and when the sun, rising over Calabria, gives a rosy color to the slope up to the snow-line, one gazes, forgetting the theatre in the glory of the mountain.

Although we had studied the theatre adequately on the first day, we were caught by the charm of the place; and a second sunrise in the theatre seemed so desirable that we broke our carefully drawn up itinerary at the very outset, the necessary two-thirds vote being easily obtained. About a thousand feet above Taormina rises a height which once served as an acropolis to ancient Tauromenium, crowned with a village and castle called Mola. Having climbed this in the hot afternoon we saw, about another thousand feet above us, a point called Monte Venere, which seemed to dominate the whole region. We subsequently read in Frances Elliot's "Travels in Sicily," "Certain misguided travellers have even been known to attempt Monte Venere." But not suspecting at the time that we were misguided, but only questioning whether the scaling of Monte Venere would cost us our table d'hôte dinner at the Hotel Timeo, we decided, by a rather doubtful two-thirds vote, to try it. We stormed it at a pace such as the Bavarian division struck at Speicheren when told that a fresh keg of beer was to be broached "up there" at ten o'clock, and that they must be on hand. As the result of our toil we got a superb view into the interior, including a peep in behind Ætna, which from this point seemed even grander than from Taormina. It was labor well spent.

During our whole stay at Taormina there was no spot on which my eye and my thoughts so frequently rested as on the little tongue of land just below us to the south, which we had passed in coming from Catania. On this vine-covered plain once lay Naxos, settled by men from Chalkis in 734 B.C. What a chain of consequences followed upon this small beginning! Leontini and Catania were founded from Naxos itself almost immediately afterward. Dorian Corinth, following hard after Ionian Chalkis, founded Syracuse, and with the birth of western Hellas the strife of Dorian and Ionian was made a part of its life. But before this strife brought ruin a period of expansion and prosperity followed which finds its only parallel in the two centuries and a half of the history of our own country.

Having no desire to traverse again a bad road, we took an early train, which brought us back to Catania at eight o'clock. Our first visit there was to the "divine artificer," who found eight punctures impartially distributed over my two tires. We thus learned to know the cactus in a new light. Hereafter we avoided even a dry piece of it lying in the road as cavalry would avoid caltrops. We took advantage of the necessary delay to visit the most interesting monument of Greek Catania, the theatre, covered by lava, on which rest the houses of the modern city. Enough underground excavation has been done to enable one to realize the appearance of the place when Alcibiades here harangued the Catanians to bring them over to the Athenian alliance, and had such drastic force lent to his lisping oratory by a body of Athenian hoplites, who, coming from their camp outside the city, broke down a weak spot in the wall and entered the city before he got to his peroration.

Again it was about noon when we mounted with intention to ride to Lentini, somewhat over a third of the way to Syracuse, across a level plain, and then take a train across the hill-country to within ten miles of Syracuse, there to resume our ride. For an hour or more we were passing through the famous "Campi Læstrygonii," which Cicero calls "*uberrima pars Siciliæ*," now known as the plain of Catania, the most extensive plain in Sicily. Then we crossed the Symæthos, and soon began a gentle climb, with the sun almost in the zenith. Now and then a turn in the road, or if not that, a look over the shoulder, gave us a fine view of Ætna, which kept increasing in majesty as we receded from it. I was thankful that we had not climbed it. That would have in some measure vulgarized it. A geologist might do it in the line of his profession. But one who wishes to keep the Ætna of Æschylus and Pindar may do better to gaze with awe from the hill of Syracuse, as *they* did, upon this Greek Sinai. I do not want to overpower a mountain like that. I want it to overpower me. One may doubt whether Coleridge would or could have written his hymn to Mont Blanc if he had "conquered" it, as tourists express it.

Just as the train for Syracuse was coming in we reached Lentini station, and this time the sea that "washes away all human ills" was not available. We here made a resolve to do our work in the future when the sun was nearer the horizon. There was nothing of interest for us to investigate in the city of Gorgias, the sophist and orator, whose silver tongue, combined with a bold and transparent trick of the Segestans, duped the Athenians, who thought themselves the wisest of men, into the Sicilian expedition. We were accordingly glad to speed along to Priolo, a station between the ruins of Megara and the flat peninsula, Thapsos. Just beyond the latter, having ridden long enough to get up steam, we washed away our ills for that day with the hill of Syracuse looking down upon us, and then as renewed men passed, when the sun was approaching the horizon, over that historic hill, and looked down on the historic harbor and on little Ortygia, large enough to hold the modern city as it held the first Corinthian colony. What a tide of associations rush over one at this sight! In a sense we were at our goal. Had we closed our journey with that nightfall we should at least have read our Thucydides for the future with different eyes.

In an exaltation of spirit we came to the Casa Politi, almost at the point of Ortygia, looking out upon the sea, where we found a German host and hostess. After our strenuous and partially successful wrestling with Italian, which had generally ended by our falling back on the member who had taken Italian at Harvard to straighten out for us the tangled web of the dialogue, how welcome it was when we asked the question, *"Haben Sie vielleicht gutes Bier?"* to get straight from the shoulder the honest answer, *"Jawohl, gewiss,"* and the more tangible answer of three foaming mugs from a cool cellar. We had lived in the spirit a good deal that day, enjoying the beauty of Taormina, Ætna, and Syracuse, and holding converse with Alcibiades and Gorgias and Thucydides. Now we hobnobbed with Gambrinus, and enjoyed "the warmest welcome in an inn."

I have never had more full and exhilarating days than those four days in Syracuse, days full of revelation, recollection, reverie, or, to put it more prosaically, days devoted to study in history and topography. The ruins of Syracuse are not to the casual observer very imposing. One might almost say of them, *"periere etiamque ruinæ."* But even these ruins have great interest for the archæologist. There is, for example, an old temple near the northern end of Ortygia, for the most part embedded in the buildings of the modern city, yet with its east end cleared and showing several entire columns with a part of the architrave upon them. And what a surprise here awaits one who thinks of a Doric temple as built on a stereotyped plan! Instead of the thirteen columns on the long sides which one is apt to look for as going with a six-column front, here are eighteen or nineteen, it is not yet quite certain which. The columns stand less than their diameter apart, and the abaci are so broad that they nearly touch. So small is the intercolumnar space that archæologists incline to the belief that in this one Doric temple there were triglyphs only over the columns, and not also between them as in all other known cases. Everything about this temple stamps it as the oldest in Sicily. An inscription on the top step, in very archaic letters, much worn and difficult to read, contains the name of Apollo in the ancient form, Ἀπέλονι. The inscription may, of course, be later than the temple; but it is in itself old enough to warrant the supposition that the temple was erected soon after the first Corinthian colonists established themselves in the island. While the inscription makes it reasonably certain that the temple belonged to Apollo, the god under whose guiding hand all these Dorians went out into these western seas, tradition, with strange perversity, has given it the name of "Temple of Diana." But it is all in the family. Whether tradition has also erred in naming the temple on the highest part of the island, into which the cathedral has been so immured that the old temple columns protrude on each side of the church, the "Temple of Minerva," is a question to which archæologists have not yet returned a unanimous answer. Indications point rather to Zeus. This temple owes its preservation, such as it is, to this immuring of the cathedral in it. In fact, the temple is nearly all present, although one might almost pass it by in the daytime without seeing it. Another temple ruin on the edge of the plateau, which begins about two miles south of the city, across the Anapos, one might also easily overlook in a casual survey, because it consists only of two columns without capitals, and a broad extent of the foundations from which the accumulated earth has been only partially removed. This was the famous temple of Olympian Zeus, built probably in the days of Hiero I., soon after the Persian war, but on the site of a temple still more venerable. One seeks a reason for the location of this holy place at such a distance from the city. Holm, the German historian of Sicily, argues with some plausibility that this was no mere suburb of Syracuse, but the original Syracuse itself. In the first place, the list of the citizens of Syracuse was kept here down at least to the time of the Athenian invasion. In the second place, tradition, which, when rightly consulted, tells so much, says that Archias, the founder of Syracuse, had two daughters, Ortygia and Syracusa, which may point to two co-ordinate settlements, Ortygia and Syracuse; the latter, which was on this temple plateau, being subsequently merged in the former, but, as sometimes happens in such cases, giving its name to the combined result.

Besides these temple ruins there are many more foundations that tell a more or less interesting story. Then there are remains of the ancient city that can never be ruined: for instance, the great stone quarries, pits over a hundred feet deep and acres broad, in some of which the Athenian prisoners were penned up to waste away under the gaze of the pitiless captors; the Greek theatre, cut out of the solid rock; the great altar of Hiero II., six hundred feet long and about half as broad, also of solid rock. Then there is the mighty Hexapylon, which closed the fortifications of Dionysius at the northwest at the point where they challenged attack from the land side. With its sally-ports and rock-hewn passages, some capacious enough to quarter regiments of cavalary, showing holes cut in the projecting corners of rock, through which the hitch-reins of the horses were wont to be passed, and its great magazines, it stands a lasting memorial to the energy of a tyrant. But while this fortress is practically indestructible, an impregnable fortress is a dream incapable of realization. Marcellus and his stout Romans came in through these fortifications, not entirely, it is true, by their own might, but by the aid of traitors, against whom no walls are proof.

One of the stone quarries, the Latomia del Paradiso, has an added interest from its association with the tyrant who made himself hated as well as feared, while Gelon was only feared without being hated. An inner recess of the quarry is called the "Ear of Dionysius," and tradition says that at the inner end of this recess either he or his creatures sat and listened to the murmurs that the people uttered against him, and that these murmurs were requited with swift and fatal punishment. Certain it is that a whisper in this cave produces a wonderful resonance, and a pistol-shot is like the roar of a cannon; but that people who had anything to say against the butcher should come up within ear-shot of him to utter it is not very likely. Historians are not quite sure that the connection of Dionysius with this recess is altogether mythical, but that he shaped it with the fell purpose above mentioned is not to be thought of, as the whole quarry is older than his time, and was probably, with the Latomia dei Cappuccini, a prison for the Athenians.

STONE QUARRY AT SYRACUSE CALLED LATOMIA DEI CAPPUCCINI

No object is more frequently mentioned in connection with Syracuse than Arethusa, the nymph changed into a fountain when pursued across the sea by the river Alpheius. The water of this fountain, much praised in antiquity, has in recent times become brackish by the letting in of salt water through earthquakes. But what it has lost in real excellence it has gained in stylish appearance. For the sake of its ancient renown, washerwomen have recently been excluded from it, a fine wall put about it, and papyrus plants added to make it look picturesque. Enveloped in a more natural beauty lies the rival fountain, Kyane, the source of the southern branch of the Anapos some distance south of the Olympieum. The nymph Kyane was turned into a fountain by Pluto because she told Demeter of the rape of Persephone. We gave half a day to Kyane, and had ourselves pushed up a stream lined with reeds and papyrus, the latter a reminder of Saracen occupation, to this spring, from which the stream comes forth with a rush. It is difficult to decide which is more beautiful, the clear, deep, broad spring or the stream through which one approaches it. The whole journey is like an excursion into fairy-land, the outside world being shut out by the reeds and papyrus.

But if the monuments of Syracuse are on the whole comparatively unimpressive, what a history is crowded into the less than three centuries between Gelon, the second founder of the city, in that he made it great, and Marcellus. This history is far from being a mere record of slaughter, and sieges, and sack of cities. The time of Hiero I. is memorable for the appearance at Syracuse, in familiar if not always friendly converse, of Pindar, Simonides, Bacchylides, Æschylus, Epicharmos and Xenophanes. One must not think of the poetry of this Hieronian circle as exotic because most of the poets were transplanted: to the Greek poets any place in the Greek world where they were appreciated and cared for was home. Anacreon sang as well and as naturally at Samos and Athens as at his native Teos; Simonides's muse was apparently equally happy in Athens, Thessaly, and Sicily; and even the Theban eagle suffered no relaxation of his wings at the Syracusan court; nay, he appears to have made his loftiest flights there. Over one-third of his epinicion odes are for Sicilian victors. Of the Titan Æschylus alone of that company one may suspect that, although he did not always get on well at home, yet the sojourn so far from Eleusis and Marathon found him homesick and heartsick. It is only rarely in the world's history that such a lot of stars gather around a court. It is a good deal that Syracuse was again visited by the muses in the time of Hiero II., when Theocritus took up his abode there.

The afternoon before we left Syracuse we got a reminder that its greatness did not all pass away with the Roman occupation. The enormous catacombs from Christian times speak of new and better days. But what stirs one more is one particular spot in the crypt of St. Marcian, a church partly made out of a temple of Bacchus. Here, in front of an old altar, a block of stone is pointed out as the stone on which St. Paul stood when he preached at Syracuse. One gets impatiently sceptical about traces of the saints in Italy; but why not accept the report that in his three days' stay at Syracuse, recorded in the Acts of the Apostles, St. Paul preached here? What is more fitting than that, by the very altar of the god of revelry, the great apostle should speak as he spoke at Athens? At any rate, I add this spot to Appii Forum and Tres Tabernæ as a place where I trod in the footsteps of a man beside whom Gelon, Pyrrhus, and Hannibal were pygmies.

II

On the journey from Syracuse to Girgenti by rail through the heart of Sicily the most interesting point is Castrogiovanni, the ancient Enna, called the navel of Sicily, a height from which one sees mountains diverging in every direction, a real *Knotenpunkt*. The railroad affords a view of Enna only from some distance as it plunges into a long tunnel under the ridge joining this height to another almost as high, on which stands Calascibetta. The surroundings of the old Sikel town, Enna, which, being early colonized by Syracuse, became a lasting monument of Greek domination over the Sikel, were probably much more beautiful in ancient times. On these rather bare heights there was once such luxuriant growth of woods and flowers that hunting-dogs lost the scent of the game. In this flower-garden the Sicilian legend placed the rape of Persephone.

As the train approached Girgenti it passed through the great sulphur region of the world. Here thousands of boys, many of them under ten years of age, carry the sulphur up to the surface. These boys are bound over by their parents to the overseers of the mines for the sum of two hundred francs, more or less, which they are expected to work off. But it takes years to do it, and many die before they succeed. The parents spend the purchase money and the children live on in despair. Our informant, a German-American, who had come over to study the sulphur industry, and who was not a sentimentalist, said that the sight of these boys going up and down the ladders with tears rolling down their cheeks had made him join in their sighs and carry a heavy heart all the way to Palermo.

The case of Girgenti is that of Syracuse reversed. Its history is not so very important, but its ruins are impressive. Even at Himera, where Theron and Akragas stood by Gelon and Syracuse, it was in a second rôle. On that occasion, when the larger part of the Carthaginian prisoners fell to Akragas, apparently because they strayed into Akragantine territory after the battle, some of the citizens are said to have got five hundred slaves apiece. From this time Akragas gave itself up to the amassing of wealth. As a consequence it became the least martial and most luxurious of Greek cities, showing, like Corinth, that a Dorian city, when once given over to pleasure, could outdo the Ionians in that direction. While Syracuse battled with Athens, Akragas remained neutral. About the only form of strenuous activity to which it arose was athletics; and even then a victory was made an occasion for a display of wealth. When Exænetos won in the stadion at Olympia, three hundred span of milk-white horses accompanied him into the city.

The luxury of Akragas took on a peculiarly showy and almost gross type. The men loaded themselves with gold ornaments. They erected tombs to horses which had won Olympic victories and to other favorite animals. A typical Akragantine was Gellias, who used to have slaves stand at his door and invite every passing stranger to come in; and once, when five hundred knights from Gela made a visit to Akragas in the winter, he took them all in, entertained them, and gave each of them a new chiton and himation. That the means of entertainment did not fail him is shown by the statement that he had three hundred rock-hewn wine-barrels, holding each a hundred amphoræ, and a big vat holding a thousand amphoræ, out of which these were filled; and this was *private* hospitality.

One could hardly expect moderation when such bountiful provision for carousal was at hand. Athenæus tells a story showing how well the young men lived up to their privileges. Some of these, drinking themselves dizzy at a banquet, declared that the house rocked like a ship, and, as if to avert impending shipwreck, began to lighten ship by pitching the furniture out of the windows, to the danger, and then to the hilarious delight, of the passers-by. But as a crowd and some disorder resulted, the generals went to the house to investigate the matter. The young bloods were equal to the emergency. They accosted the graybeards as Tritons, thanked them for deliverance from the storm, and vowed to sacrifice to them so soon as they had got over their sea-sickness and fright. The old men, being carried away with the humor of the thing, entered into the spirit of the joke, and that house was ever after known as "the ship."

Such a joke might have been played in a good many other towns, but the following bit of gossip, if not true, is *ben trovato*, and has a peculiarly Akragantine flavor. It is related that at the fatal siege of the city by the Carthaginians, when all was at stake, a law was passed restricting the guards when at their posts to one under-mattress and one over-mattress, one blanket, and two pillows. If these things were done in a green tree, what was done in a dry? Empedocles, the most eminent citizen of Akragas, said of his fellow-citizens that they indulged in high living as if they were going to die to-morrow, but built as if they were going to live forever. The first half of this statement we have to judge by gossip, which, as it is very bulky and all to the same point, may well make us believe that when there is so much smoke there must be some fire. For the corroboration of the latter half, go to Girgenti and *circumspice*.

What a moment was that when, toward the end of the afternoon, after toiling up from the station on the north side of Girgenti to the city itself, which occupied the site of the acropolis of Akragas, we looked down on the plateau sloping southward toward the sea, and dotted with the famous ruins long known to us by photographs. About a mile below us, in the direction of the ruins, was the Hôtel des Temples, which we had been told in Syracuse was to close for the summer the day before. But as "the Greeks got into Troy by trying," we thought we would try to get into this hotel, and be near our goal. At the door a boy declared that the house was closed; but at our request he said he would call the padrone. In ten minutes there appeared in riding clothes, and leading a horse, the most charming landlord of Sicily, with a bewitching smile and the manners of a gentleman. He said that, although his house was closed and his cook gone, he had not the heart to send us back up into the city. We could have, he said, eight or nine beds apiece, and, as he had a hunting comrade with him for the night, he could give us some soup and meat.

More than satisfied to have established a base of operations, without a delay of five minutes we were at the Concordia Temple, the most perfectly preserved Greek temple, unless we except perhaps the Theseum. Having an hour and a half of daylight, we used it in getting a first view of nearly everything on the plateau, and then returned to what we supposed was to be a frugal meal. But the dinner was an Akragantine feast, the best of the whole journey, with the possible exception of the next one at the same table. We wondered what sort of a dinner the regular cook would have produced if this was done by a novice; and when the padrone made apologies for his dinner, we searched his smiling face for traces of sarcasm.

The next day we enjoyed in detail what we had already enjoyed in the lump, that row of temples lined up along the southern edge of the plateau which here ends in a rocky precipice. These temples when new, with the city of half a million inhabitants behind it, and the acropolis above it with still more temples, must have been a very effective sight to one coming up from the sea five miles away.

SO-CALLED CONCORDIA TEMPLE AT GIRGENTI

Although the material of the temples is a friable yellow sandstone, quarried near by, we must not in reconstructing our picture think of them as yellow temples. They doubtless had stucco and paint enough to hide this core. The stone is so porous that it is not surprising to find the columns on the south side—*i.e.*, the side most exposed to the sirocco—badly eaten away. The whole line dates from the fifth century, and was doubtless planned and begun by Theron, who had armies of slaves from Himera.

What Greek name the Concordia Temple had is unknown. Holm suspects that it is the temple of Demeter, although the substructure under a church farther up the hill has generally been assigned to her. It owes its excellent preservation to the fact that in the Middle Ages it was turned into a church of St. Gregory of the turnips, whoever he was, when the cella walls were perforated with a series of arches on each side, to let in the light.

The next best preserved is the temple of Hera Lacinia, in the most commanding situation of all, having the precipice, which is here higher and more abrupt, on its east front, as well as on its south side. It is also considerably the highest of the line. Its present name is surely wrong. It is quite likely to have been a temple of Poseidon, a divinity held in honor at Akragas, a horse-rearing as well as a maritime city. The temple of Herakles is more interesting than either of these, although only one column stands upright; the rest lie as they were thrown down by an earthquake, in such good order that it would be easy to set them up again; and the result would be much more important than Cavalari's so-called temple of Castor and Pollux, which, being a corner of a temple put together out of two different temples, should be properly called "Cavalari's folly." The temple of Herakles is rightly named. It was identified as being at the sacred gate and near the agora. It is much larger than the two temples already described, and shows, like them, traces of a great conflagration which reddened the yellow stone in places. Its ground plan is very clear but peculiar, and so extremely interesting. Sicily is the place of all others to study the construction of the Greek temple.

But the object of greatest interest is the Zeus Temple, still farther west in the line. This justifies the saying of Empedocles above quoted, being so large that the Parthenon could be lost in one corner of it, as the wooden ladle was lost in Lady Wouter Van Twiller's pocket. It is the most massive of Greek temples, in the sense in which the temple of Zeus at Olympia is more massive than the Parthenon—*i.e.*, its columns and all its members are larger. So enormous were its dimensions that the architect readily saw that he must deviate from the ordinary rules of construction. Columns of friable stone fifty-five feet high, supporting an unusually heavy entablature, needed support themselves. Accordingly they were embedded in a continuous wall. What one here saw was not a line of graceful columns between which and the cella one could walk about, but only a great wall with half columns protruding from it. These half columns were not really independent members. The small blocks composing them run over into the wall to the right and left. They simply serve to break up a monotonous wall, and to present the appearance of columns. This contour, which is a little over a semi-circumference, averages about twenty feet, being, of course, greater at the bottom. A man's back, as was remarked by Diodorus Siculus, easily fits into the flutings. The clearest idea, however, of the large proportions of the temple I got by noting that the grooves in a triglyph lying on the ground measured fifteen feet in length. It would also be no exaggeration to say that a company could dance on the top of one of the capitals lying about.

The inside of this temple must have been as peculiar as the outside. The great question here is where to place the gigantic figures called Atlantes or Telamones, male figures corresponding to the female figures on the Erechtheum, but, unlike them, showing exertion, like Atlas in the Olympia metope. Probably they stood on the lateral walls of the cella, and, with their twenty-five feet, they would reach up to the roof, like the second row of columns at Pæstum. The cella probably ran clear through from one end of the temple to the other, and, while the two divisions of the temple to the right and left of it, which were as much closed as the cella itself, had entrances from the east, the cella was probably entered from the west. One has to say "probably" very often in speaking of the interior, because the temple has been nearly all carried away to make the pier at Porto Empedocle, the harbor of the modern city. As late as 1401 three columns were still standing and carrying a piece of the architrave. But the temple entered very early on the stage of dilapidation, for the reason that the roof was never put upon it. For more than half a century, even from the time of Theron, Akragas had wrought upon this monster building, and had not finished it when the Carthaginian fury broke upon her. Although the city rose again, and even prospered, it never saw a day for taking up again such a gigantic enterprise.

Besides this temple of Olympian Zeus there was an older temple of Zeus Polieus on the acropolis, to which an unusual interest attaches, because it was built by Phalaris, of execrable memory, who, having attached to himself a band of laborers for the construction of the temple, by their help seized the sovereign power and subverted the democracy. Down in the crypt of the Church of Santa Maria dei Greci we were shown a regular stylobate of three steps, and on the top step eight columns, the upper parts of which run up into the church, which shows also columns of the other long side of the temple. Tradition claims this as the identical temple built by Phalaris. But as the forms of the columns forbid putting them back into the sixth century we do better to identify them with the temple of Athena on the acropolis. The temple built by Phalaris is to be sought, then, on the ground occupied by the modern cathedral. Jove gave place to Jesus, and the virgin goddess, as at Athens, to the Virgin Mother.

When we told our smiling host that we intended to ride in one day from his hotel to Castelvetrano, the point of departure for Selinus, he said the thing was impossible. We told him that, while we admitted his judgment in all that pertained to horses, we were going to make the sixty-two miles which, according to Baedeker, lay between us and our goal between sunrise and sunset, however bad the road might be. He then, like a true sportsman, got interested, offered to bet, and when we declined begged us to telegraph back to him if we really did it.

As we had to wake up the cook the next morning, after waking up ourselves, the sun was well up in the heavens before we got off. But the coffee which cost us so much time must have told on our gait; for a fellow-countryman, whom we first met two days later at Palermo, seemed impressed by it, and rather proud of it. He asked, "Didn't I see you go through Porto Empedocle the day before yesterday morning on bicycles?" When we assented he said: "Well, I told the American Consul who was with me, 'I bet dose vas American boys.'" And the next day he repeated, as if pleased with his own sagacity, "I told the Consul, 'I bet dose vas American boys.'"

As we started the next morning toward Selinus, after passing the night at Castelvetrano, I realized that this, more even than Syracuse, was my chief object of interest in this long-delayed Sicilian journey.

The history of this short-lived colony of a colony is invested with a pathetic interest. Planted by Sicilian Megara in 628 B.C., as an outpost of Hellas toward the west, it was a standing challenge to the Phœnicians. But there was not always war between Hellas and Canaan. The Phœnicians, who had long been in possession of the west end of the island, were bent on gain, while the Greek sought rather for a free unfolding of his civic life; and so, Selinus, with a little temporizing, got on with its neighbors.

There were some strange vicissitudes in Sicilian politics. From the time when Carthage appeared in Sicily as a protector of the older Phœnician settlements, Selinus saw its advantage in siding with her against other rivals. On the great day of Himera, Gelon and Theron had to contend against Selinus as well as against Carthage. This off-side play was not, however, regarded by the other Sicilian cities as sufficient cause for shutting Selinus out of the sisterhood of states.

But, while Selinus had an eye to profit, it did not, like Akragas, forget the art of war. That she was a power in western Sicily in the days when Carthage was so strangely inactive for seventy years after Himera, is shown by an inscription of this time, which mentions a victory won by the Selinuntians "with the aid of Zeus and Phobos and Herakles and Apollo and Poseidon and the Tyndaridæ and Athena and Malophoros and Pasikrateia and the other gods, but especially Zeus." This drawing in of so large a part of the pantheon implies that it was a great victory. Probably it was won from Segesta, that most hated Elymian neighbor. But Segesta knew how to help herself. After she had lured Athens to destruction in this same quarrel, she invoked the Carthaginian on a mission of destruction. For the Carthaginian was not subdued, but was biding his time, and, when he again fell upon Sicily, it was his old ally, Selinus, that first felt the weight of his arm. Then Zeus and Phobos seemed to forsake her. But her conduct was such in that awful visitation that Hellas had no reason to blush for this daughter.

The force which Hannibal led against her was, at the lowest estimate, 100,000, which was more than the total population of the city. The first attack on the land side, where the walls were weak and out of repair because no danger had threatened for years, was repulsed. A call for help was sent to both Akragas and Syracuse. The former might have had its contingent before the walls in three days, allowing one for the messenger. But Akragas waited for the Syracusans, who were two days farther off, to come and take them on the way. She paid the penalty for this delay three years later. She, as well as Syracuse, ought to have known that at Selinus they would be fighting for their own life. Syracuse was, moreover, an ally of Selinus in the war against Athens, which was finished only three years before with such eclat as to make Syracuse a proper champion of the Greek cities against the great enemy.

It is probable that the call for help was sent out before the enemy actually made its assault, but so speedy were the movements of the Carthaginians that one might have expected even prompt aid to come too late. Selinus, however, held out with such tenacity as to frustrate all calculation. For nine days, in the consciousness that she stood as a vanguard of Hellas, while the eastern hills were eagerly scanned for the succor that was hourly expected, Selinus conducted a defence rarely equalled in history.

There were not men enough to allow reliefs in defending the wall. The same men stood at their posts day and night. The old men brought new weapons, and sharpened those that were dull. The women carried food and water. Even on the ninth day, when the fierce Iberian mercenaries broke through the wall and the weary defenders, and got inside the city, the defence did not cease. The city had to be taken house by house, men and women hurling down stones from the house-tops until the supply was exhausted. And now, house after house was pillaged by men spurred on by the promise of free plunder given by Hannibal; and delicate women fell into hands compared with which the claws of wild beasts were tender. Soldiers paraded the streets with heads on the points of their spears and strings of hands slung over their shoulders. Only 2,600 survivors somehow found their way to Akragas.

On this very day a large force started from Syracuse; but when, united with the contingent of Akragas, it confronted the Carthaginians, the woe of Selinus was accomplished. Hannibal told these belated allies that he had dealt Selinus only its deserts, and that even its gods had pronounced against it. What a theme for a Jeremiah!

The six large temples of Selinus lie in a worse condition than that in which the Carthaginians left them. Earthquakes have been more active here than at Akragas. But these ruins, in two large groups, one on the acropolis and one on a plateau to the east, are the most interesting, as well as the most impressive, ruins in Europe. Their interest lies in the fact that they present us in tangible form the history of Greek architecture as it unfolded itself in a provincial town. There is Temple C (probably a Herakles temple; but archæologists have refrained from giving doubtful names, and designated the temples by letters. Perhaps the names given at Syracuse and Girgenti, though false, are better pegs to serve the memory than letters), with "shapeless sculpture," the well-known metope representing Perseus cutting off the head of Medusa, and another with Heracles carrying the mischievous Kerkopes flung over his shoulder. These grotesque attempts at sculpture, as well as the general consideration that the first thought of a colony was to erect a temple, allow us to date this oldest temple of Selinus as early as 600 B.C. The architecture is vastly better than the sculpture, a complete Doric style, with something of the clumsiness which marks the venerable ruin at Corinth. Then we may notice Temple E, probably a Hera temple, the southernmost of the three on the eastern plateau, a large and beautiful temple, once most gorgeously painted, and giving us, perhaps, more light than any other temple on the subject of polychromy in Doric architecture. The metopes, the best of which is Zeus receiving Hera on Mount Ida, mark this temple as a product of the early part of the fifth century, about the time of the temple of Zeus at Olympia. Then, at the other end of this line, on the eastern plateau, is Temple G, so enormous that it is supposed, like its brother at Akragas, to have been meant for none other than Zeus, the King of the gods. It is a few feet longer and a few feet wider than the great Akragas temple. Its date is given with a melancholy certainty; for it, as well as the Akragas temple, was never finished. It may well have taken a small community like this as much as the "forty and six years" which the Temple of Jerusalem required to put up such a colossal building. An especial interest attaches to it because we see it, as it were, stopped midway in a lively process of coming into being. Some of the huge drums are combined into columns, a few of which are fluted from top to bottom, while others have a little start of fluting at the top and bottom, and still others are only cut in the form of a twenty-sided polygon. But one must go to Campo Bello, about five miles distant, to feel in a still more lively manner the interruption of the building process. Here one sees a cliff where in one case workmen had just marked out, with a circular groove, a column-drum to be detached from its bed. In another place is one around which workmen have hewn for months, so that it is almost ready to be detached. Hard by are some already detached and rolled a little distance toward Selinus; still others are found transported half-way or more to the temple. The people of the country are filled with wonder at the sight. They recognize the fact that all these blocks were meant for the great temple; and some of them told an early traveller that the women of Selinus used to carry these stones on their heads from the quarry to the temple, spinning flax all the way as they went, adding, with naïveté: "But, you know, it was a race of women much larger than ours."

These interesting temples show, as they stand side by side, great freedom in the application of the rules of Doric style. For instance, the number of columns on the side of a hexastyle temple varies from thirteen to seventeen. The number of steps also varies from two to six, instead of the canonical three.

When we visited Segesta the next day and saw its temple, also unfinished, as it was when the city was stricken down by the Greek Agathocles, we felt little pity for this city which had stirred up so much mischief for its foe, Selinus, and for its friend, Athens. But perhaps, after all, this Elymian city's greatest crime was saying, "I must live." If Selinus refused to accept this proposition, Segesta called in Athens or Carthage, regardless of the woes that might in consequence come upon those who disputed her right to live.

In shooting down from Segesta to the northern shore, without further exploration of what may be called the country of Æneas, we got glimpses of Mount Eryx, the favorite haunt of Venus; and later in the day the train brought us to Palermo, "that wonderful cross-section of history." But as it was not rich in Greek history our tour in western Hellas was at an end.

DALMATIA

June, lovely June, has been the bringer of two good things to me—Sicily and the Dalmatian coast; and now that the charm of the latter is fresh it seems almost to outshine the former.

When I came on board the Austrian Lloyd steamer Galatea at Corfu I had little idea of what awaited me. One reads of this "Norway of the South," this "Switzerland in the sea"; but how little these comparisons convey until the landscape has really been seen. My main purpose was rest from the heat of Greece, and a more or less careful study of the ruins of Spalato.

This Dalmatian line is adapted to one who wishes to travel lazily. The stops as far as Spalato are longer than the passages; the boat, however, starts in each case promptly according to the schedule. The only exception was at Corfu; when all was ready, and we were just about to hoist the anchor, a Greek boatman came up alongside with a barge loaded with casks and boxes. It was so characteristic of a Greek.

While we were moving along the coast of Albania until late in the afternoon, there was nothing new to look out for; and so there was time to get acquainted with the ship and the passengers, to get one's bearings. There were the rules for passengers printed in five parallel columns—English, French, German, Italian, and Greek—emphasizing the cosmopolitan constituency of the travelling public. In Europe, and especially in the Orient, it always pays to read regulations, particularly the English column, to see how foreigners wrestle with our language. Rule 3 said: "Every damage is to be made good by the person who *dit* it." Rule 11: "It is prohibited to any passenger to *middle* with the command and direction of the vessel." As I had always trusted to the captain to run his own ship, I felt safe on that point. Particular anxiety for the ladies ran through the rules. One rule was: "Gentlemen are not allowed to enter the cabins of the ladies," and as a final snapper at the end of the last rule was this sentence: "Passengers having a right to be treated like persons of education will no doubt conform themselves to the rules of good society by respecting their fellow-travellers and paying a due regard to the fair sex." As we had no ladies at all on board until the journey was about half finished it began to seem as if they had been frightened away.

The captain, like most of the captains of this line, was of Slavic origin. Of other languages than his own he knew only Italian. In this he did all his "cussing" at every port; and it seemed to produce everywhere the proper effect. His gentlest conversational tone was like the blast of a trumpet and could be heard from stem to stern. I took an early opportunity to go up to the bridge when he was there, and remark apologetically that I was travelling *per vedere qualche cosa*. His laconic reply was, *"Ma perchè no?"* With that I felt myself installed on the bridge, and I spent more hours there during the voyage than any one of the officers. Perhaps the third-class passengers standing below suspected me of attempting to "middle with the command and direction of the vessel."

Toward evening we passed Akrokeraunia, the massive headland ending off a chain of mountains back of it over six thousand feet high, in antiquity the cynosure of sailors crossing by the shortest line from Italy to Greece. The modern name, Capo Duro, suggests its pitilessness. There it stands running out to the northwest, and so bidding defiance to the strongest wind of the region. The sea has beaten against it since there was a sea; it has broken away a good deal of it, if we may judge by a single isolated island thrown out in front of it. The high mountains seem saying to the sea, "You waste your vain fury on those lower rocks. What will you do when you come to us?" But it is the business of the patient sea to help "draw down the Aonian hills," and until there shall be no more sea Capo Duro must yield inch by inch.

Having passed Akrokeraunia, we turned sharply to the right, and changed our course from north to south until we dropped anchor in the harbor of Valona. As far as Cattaro the chief function of our boat was the transportation of freight, and that was the reason why the stops were so long. The captain was an ardent fisherman; hardly was the anchor down when his little boat dropped astern, and he fished sometimes far on into the night. He counted his catch not by numbers, but by kilos; and since the other officers in a circle around the stern, leaning over the taffrail, vied with the captain, fish were plentiful on board. All along this shore were great forests of holm-oak, and the cargo that we took on here was almost entirely valonia, so much used in Europe by tanners.

In the night we got off, and I missed the site of the great ancient city Apollonia, a little to the north of our stopping-place. But in the forenoon we stopped at Durazzo, the ancient Dyrrhachium, which, situated at the beginning of the great Via Egnatia, saw the passage of so many Roman armies into Greece. Cæsar and Pompey passed that way to their great struggle for the possession of the world. In earlier days it was known under the name of Epidamnos, as the colony of Kerkyra which set its mother city at war with her own mother city, Corinth, and so lighted the fire that destroyed Greece in the dreadful Peloponnesian war. At Durazzo my only first-class fellow-passenger got off.

Of third-class passengers we had a plenty, and a nondescript crowd they were; in other words, they beggared description. Some were magnificently dressed; but even those who were in rags were picturesque. If a painter had been present he would have been troubled by an *embarras de richesse*. Red and yellow were the prevailing colors in that motley crowd; gold embroidery was abundant. The few women present kept pretty well in the background, and took little or no part in the exuberant jollity of the men, who sang and danced in true Oriental style, keeping for the most part a somewhat monotonous droning, but rising sometimes into frenzy. This, continued far on into the evening hours, was bewitching. The situation was, or at least seemed to be, made for my special benefit. I seemed to have a private steamer, with the captain and crew working for me, and these fantastic and jolly people amusing me, who had promised not even "to *middle*."

But the next day I was brought from reverie to my senses by the coming of first-class passengers. At Dulcino, the first of the two harbors recently gained by Montenegro, which thus became a maritime state, the Mayor of the town came on board to travel *via* Cattaro up to Cettinje, the capital, a long way around, but the way of least resistance. *He* did not break the charm, for a more gorgeously dressed and finer-shaped man one seldom sees. Scores of Montenegrins of the singers and dancers of the preceding evening, cooks and gardeners returning to their homes from Constantinople, where they are in great demand, crowded around this magnate and kissed his hand in true Oriental style, which he took in patriarchal fashion. This was in keeping with the scenes of the day before; but this giant's wife and children were nothing but ordinary, plain people. At the next port, Antivari, a regular European lady, the wife of the Lloyd agent, came on board with the whole population of the village to give her a send-off; and we at once stepped out of dream-land.

I now fell into another mood. The whole voyage, with its long and frequent stops, began to seem a regular lark, and I so entered into the spirit of the thing that I determined at the next stop to get my bicycle up out of the hold and get a little acquaintance with the country which lay back of the long mountain line of coast. As we were booked to stop at Cattaro forty-four and a half hours, that seemed a good place to begin. The big Montenegrins had interested me so much I would go up and see where such fellows grew.

Who can describe the Gulf, or, as they call it there, the Bocche di Cattaro? It enjoys the distinction of being "perhaps the finest harbor in the world." There is a break in the coast line; as you go in you find yourself in a broad bay; but that is not all; you pass through another opening, into another bay, and so on, the mountains growing higher all the time until, by passing five channels, one so narrow that it used to be stopped by a chain, and so is called to-day Catena, you reach the fifth bay, on the east shore of which, nestled up against the base of a high dark mountain, one of those from which the region Montenegro got its name, lies Cattaro, a town of five or six thousand inhabitants, the outpost of Austria to the south. For a brief period at about the end of the Napoleonic wars, Montenegro held this place and the Bocche.

No doubt all Montenegrins long to possess it again; for it is their natural outlet to the sea, from which the thin line of Austria here shuts them out, except for the poor harbors farther south.

Much history has been enacted around this gulf, which was a prize too valuable not to be striven for. In fact, it is a paradise like few on earth. All the way through the devious passages one is reminded of Lake Lucerne by the mountain banks and of Como by the tropical vegetation. Many of the officers of the Austrian Lloyd have their homes on these shores. Our captain and at least one of the other officers spent two days here with their families. The latter brought back word that an American king named Morgan had just visited the Bocche on his yacht.

CATTARO

We arrived shortly after noon; but it took me just an hour and a half to get my bicycle through the custom-house. The officials hardly knew what to do with it. Probably no bicycle had ever entered that port, and it may be a long time before another enters. I have no doubt that they thought me a fool for bringing mine in; and one could hardly blame them for the thought. The Austrian officials, however, are so affable—I have never met an exception—that one cannot think of losing his own patience. In the cool of the day, in order to test the road, I walked, with a very little riding, up the zigzag road, getting a little taste of what awaited one who would go to Cettinje, and then dropped down again in twenty minutes after the sun had gone down. I had had enjoyment enough to pay for the experiment, and had come to the

- 115 -

conclusion, on perhaps rather insufficient data, that on the next day, with good weather, I could get to Cettinje and back if I girded myself to it, so slight is the lateral distance on the map.

To make sure of the case, I rose early and left the ship at half-past four, with a cake of chocolate in my pocket, for the rest trusting to living on the country. Not until seven o'clock did the country offer anything. Then I got coffee from a Highland girl at a very primitive inn at the point of one of the zigzags. She had not "a very shower of beauty"; but she did have "the freedom of a mountaineer," and a kindly twinkle in her eye. A man takes kindly to the hand and face that signify refreshment in time of need. When I asked how far it was to Cettinje the mountain maid said "*tetre ore*," which, though it was a rather bad mixture of Italian and something else, probably Slavic, was extremely encouraging. Even if the climb continued for two hours more I ought to reduce her "four hours" to three. In fact, at eight o'clock, at the end of three and a half hours of steady toiling climb, I found myself at an altitude of nearly three thousand feet, almost perpendicularly above Cattaro, with the Galatea so near that it seemed as if I could drop a stone upon her deck; but I thought it best not to try; I was in a hurry. In a few minutes more I broke through the mountain which had given me so much trouble, and I was in Montenegro. I soon passed the frontier town of Njegus, in the bed of a dried-up lake, the birthplace of Prince Nicholas, the ruling sovereign, who has a country house there of such modest appearance that one could hardly believe it to belong to a prince.

Now my work began anew; another mountain wall confronted me and the road, which as far as the border had been good, was freshly strewn with cracked stones, the bicyclist's terror. When at last I reached the top of this second range, a sight worth seeing unfolded itself before my eye. All Montenegro, a mass of gray stone rising here and there into peaks, lay spread out before me. In the far northeast one could see the important hill fortress of Niksic, but no land anywhere appeared. In fact, all the soil in Montenegro, except in the southern part around Lake Skutari, is found in larger or smaller clefts of the rocks; Cettinje itself being simply one of the largest of these. Now it was downhill, and I abused my wheel shamefully, running it hard over the stones as the only way of accomplishing the journey. At about ten o'clock, just after feasting my eyes on the grand chain of snow-covered Illyrian mountains in the background, I turned a large cliff and looked down into a bowl five or ten times as large as that of Njegus, and saw at its farther end Cettinje, looking like a large German country village with roofs of red tiles. This is without doubt the most primitive capital of Europe. Words almost fail to express its plainness. But it is a place worth seeing, and after a reasonable halt I made haste to traverse in the blazing sun the two or three miles which lay between the rim of the bowl where I stood and the town.

It was some years since I had felt myself so out of the world as I did up there among the mountains and men of Slavic speech. I betook myself to a modest inn, Kraljevic Al Marco, for lunch. After wrestling to my satisfaction with Italian, I noticed that the landlady turned to her little boy and said something to him in Greek. Quick as a flash the ice was broken and we were talking Greek like lightning. It was a family of Greeks, the brother of the landlady being the interpreter at the Greek Consulate.

After an hour or two of rest they showed me about the town for awhile, after which I cut loose to see things for myself. What a plain town it is! The palace of the present sovereign, called the New Palace, is one of the few two-story buildings in the place, but even this has hardly any ornament except four pairs of attached Corinthian columns on each of the stories at the front side, and two pairs on each of the other sides. The so-called "Old Palace" is plainer than most modern jails. The one building of interest is the monastery, in which lies buried the ancestor of the ruling family, on whose sarcophagus the Montenegrins lay their hands and swear when they go out to battle to be good and true soldiers. And they have kept their oaths well. These Montenegrins are simply Servians who never bowed the knee to the Turks. It has occurred more than once or twice that a Turkish army has entered this land of rocks eighty thousand strong, sweeping everything before it, only to return decimated, if perchance it escaped destruction. There is a round tower in the rear of the monastery, on which the heads of Turks used to be nailed up.

It was good luck for me that my visit fell on Sunday, for the men were in their best dress. Dress did not make the man; the man was there to begin with. There was hardly an adult who did not measure over six feet; and they looked every inch a man. If there were only enough of them they would soon settle the Eastern question. Alexander III. of Russia knew how to value his "only faithful ally." In contrast to the men, the women look like drudges. The male sex has really arrogated to itself all the beauty, a result that has come about from the fact that, while the men have for ages borne arms and ranged free, the women have been the tillers of the scanty soil as well as servants of all work. *Men* are the one product of Montenegro. The only product of the *soil* beyond the grain and potatoes, which afford scanty sustenance, is tobacco, which is good and cheap. There is a heavy duty on it in Austria, something like two hundred per cent.; everybody tries to smuggle it in, and the trick often succeeds.

The next day was the birthday of the Crown Prince, and when I made ready to depart my new friends said, "Of course you are going to stay to the great festival," apparently thinking that that was what I came for. I asked if the young man himself was to be present, and they replied, "Oh! no." "Then," said I, "I think I will not be present either." So I got off at half-past two in a fierce heat, and by easy stages, meeting as I went several of my stalwart third-class fellow-passengers, I reached the Galatea in season for a good dinner.

On the way from Cattaro to Spalato the chief object of interest is Ragusa, a strongly fortified city of about twelve thousand inhabitants, which, after maintaining itself as a free republic until 1805, often leaning upon Venice the while, went in the next decade through great vicissitudes, being in 1811 annexed by Napoleon to the new "Kingdom of Illyria," and in 1814 falling into the hands of Austria, so good at taking hold but so slow at letting go. But, after all that may be said of the land-greed of Austria, it has been no evil lot for Dalmatia to fall into her hands. Austria has inherited—let Professor Freeman turn over in his grave to hear it said—the rôle of Rome as road-builder, civilizer, and introducer of general prosperity along this coast. She is now pushing a network of railroads along the coast and up from the coast towns into the interior. Ragusa has a very Venetian look in its old part and a very nineteenth-century look in its new part. Its surroundings are almost as interesting as the city itself. On the lovely island Lacroma, hard by on the south, is a church founded by Richard Cœur de Lion. Somewhat farther off to the north, on the shore, lies Canosa, ever remembered by a spring of pure water shaded by two gigantic plane-trees forty feet in circumference, an enchanted spot. At or near Ragusa lay the Greek city Epidauros.

In this region might well be located the "Islands of the Blessed"; for here we begin to encounter islands by tens and dozens, large and small. The rest of the journey was dodging in and out among islands. We have lakes in America which boast their three hundred and sixty-five islands, one for each day in the year; but the Dalmatian islands are not to be counted by hundreds, but by thousands, if one were to count them at all. They are generally spoken of as innumerable. Geologists say that there has been here a subsidence of great strips of land, and that the sea has in some cases broken up the remaining strips into pieces of a size to suit itself, ranging from fifty rods to fifty miles in length. Here comes the infinite charm of sailing along the Dalmatian coast, this interlocking of sea and shore. No wonder that the Dalmatians are all sailors, wooers of the salt sea gale. I myself longed to get off the steamer and get into one of the numerous sailboats that were ploughing through the dashing waves.

Had the Galatea stopped as long at Spalato as it had at Cattaro, I should have been tempted to crowd my enjoyment of it into the same space; but she had now transformed herself into an express boat, bent on reaching Trieste in the shortest possible time. So, with some regret, I left my hospitable quarters on my floating home to trust myself to the welcome of an inn.

But little did I care for the inn. Within a quarter of an hour from the time when I left the steamer I was in the heart of one of the strangest cities of the world, threading my way through narrow winding streets, passing here and there a temple, generally embedded in some later building, running up against a continuous wall two or three stories high which I followed until I found a gate that would let me go through it; then I followed the outside of this wall until I found another gate that let me in again, when the maze again engulfed me. I was in the famous Palace of Diocletian.

The city Spalato was once all inside the palace (palatium), and got its name from that fact; but in later years the city has so grown that the palace is embedded and almost lost in the city. In order to get a good idea of the city and palace together one should climb the campanile, a fine Romanesque structure, incomparably finer than that the loss of which Venice now mourns. In 1882 it became necessary to take down all but the four lower stories and rebuild. Money has come in slowly, and the staging which practically hides the beautiful campanile may not come down for several years more. The door leading into this immense wooden structure bore the legend, *L'ingresso è vietato*. But following a maxim hewn from life, that a sightseer must always go on until he is stopped, I went and pushed my way through the workmen, boss and all, probably with a more assured air because a good citizen had a few minutes before told me, "You will see a sign saying 'No admittance,' but it doesn't mean anything."

SPALATO. PALACE OF DIOCLETIAN. SOUTH FRONT.

At the foot of the campanile is an Egyptian sphinx whose head has been battered by a falling stone. The natives call it the "man-woman," and, curiously enough, they call the sun disk between its paws "pogazza" (a loaf of bread), a roundabout corroboration of what I used to hear in childhood: "The moon is made of green cheese; the sun's a loaf of bread." The view from the top is fine, whether you look landward or seaward; but the real reward of the climb is that here only the extent and plan of the palace and the adjustment of the buildings within it become perfectly clear.

The term "palace" is a misnomer. What we have is really an enormous enclosure, a sort of Roman camp. The area is trapezoidal; in other words, the sides vary in length. The north or landward side, which is the longest, has a length of 700 feet. The circuit is about half a mile, and it consumes the better part of half an hour to work your way around it. There could, of course, be no question of roofing over such a space. The whole area was divided into four approximately equal squares by two great passages, one thirty-six feet broad, leading from the water gate on the south side called the Silver Gate, through which the imperial barge used to sail into the palace, to the Golden Gate on the north side, the other running from the Iron Gate on the west to the Bronze Gate on the east. The first of these ways is interrupted near the south end by the imperial house itself. The enclosing wall was fifty feet high at its lowest part, and was seventy-five feet high near the sea where the ground fell off, so that all the buildings, sacred and profane, distributed within were hidden from view to outsiders. Not only did the imperial family, but courtiers and menials, making a population of some thirty thousand, have quarters here.

The builder and occupant of this palace was the greatest personality of the Cæsars after Marcus Aurelius, whom in military and administrative force he greatly surpassed. Entering the service as a simple legionary, he rose by slow degrees of service in all parts of the empire under various nonentities of emperors, until at Chalkedon, in 284 A.D., the soldiers proclaimed him emperor. There is a legend that a Druid priestess had prophesied to him when he was serving in Belgium under Aurelian that he would become emperor immediately after killing a boar. It is said that he saw the fulfilment of this prophecy when the Emperor Numerianus was assassinated at Chalkedon by a certain Aper (*i.e.*, boar), whom he immediately struck down, exclaiming, "I have killed the boar." Of course there are those who think that the legend grew out of the name of the assassin. Diocletian's name will ever be associated with the last and most wide-reaching and systematic persecution of the Christians; but this policy was most likely forced upon him by the fanaticism of his colleague, Galerius. At this time the Roman Empire had become too bulky to be well administered by one man, however able and conscientious, and of his own accord he associated others with himself in the imperial power, confining himself entirely to the eastern part. Two years after he had issued at Nikomedia, in 303 A.D., his edict of persecution of the Christians, the cares of office weighing too heavily upon him, he laid aside the purple, retired to Salona, and began building this palace about four miles distant from it. When his withdrawal was so sorely felt that he was importuned to resume the imperial power, he declined, referring to the sweet peace which he enjoyed among his cabbages at Salona. There can be little doubt that the reason which influenced him to choose Salona as his place of retirement was that it was his birthplace, although the Montenegrins hold that they have the true birthplace in Doclea, not far from Cettinje.

But the old Emperor's musings in his great palace must have been sadder than Hadrian's conversings with his soul at Tivoli. Here he learned of the triumph of Christianity through Constantine, a meaner spirit than he. Then came the overturning of his statues at Rome and the banishment and subsequent butchery of his wife and daughter. Added to all this was a painful illness; and in the eighth year of his residence in that palace where he had promised himself so much comfort and sweet peace, to adopt the words of Marcus Aurelius, that noblest Roman of them all, he "found the house smoky and went out."

Beside the pathetic interest attaching to the great founder of the palace, another interest attaches to the immuring of it in the modern city. In the seventh century Anno Domini waves of barbarians swept down along the coast of Dalmatia. One of these was composed of Avars—a people often mixed up, whether rightly or wrongly, with the Huns. Even more than the Huns they were a "scourge of God." After leaving a desert in their trail, butchering men and yoking women to their carts, they came into this lovely region, destroyed the great city, and then decided to settle down here. There was a grand scattering of the degenerate Romans, who had been unable to hold their own, to the neighboring islands, but after awhile a remnant came back and occupied the palace, which was fairly well adapted to be used as a fort. Here they defied the Avars, and at last outstayed them. The result was the present city of Spalato.

One's first impression is that the palace, although tremendously impressive from the outside wherever that is visible, has yet suffered immensely from its partial burial in the modern city. The two temples within were much more buried than the great wall, and have been only partially brought to light again. But in another aspect of the case the modern city saved the palace. Had the latter stood by itself it would have been treated as a stone quarry, like so many ancient cities, Salona itself, for example. Now there is hope that by removing here and there a modern building—a process that was begun some time ago—the greater part of the palace may be restored to the light of day. In fact, the Porta Aurea has quite recently been freed from encumbrances and, even without being restored, makes a fine impression.

From all that one now sees it is clear that the architecture, though impressive as a whole, is shabby when examined in detail. The exquisite finish of the Greek is, of course, lacking. But even compared with some other Roman work it is seen to have been hastily done. Its nearest parallel is found in Palmyra, which was restored by Diocletian.

The enclosing wall has half columns of the Doric order in a lower story and Ionic half columns in a second. Of the buildings inside, the "peristyle" in front of the royal residence makes the best impression, because the space enclosed by it was thoroughly cleared out by the Emperor Francis I. of Austria, nearly a century ago, a benefaction duly recorded on a tablet inserted in an adjacent wall. Many of the columns of the peristyle itself, however, are still half embedded in the walls of buildings too important to be torn down. A building which is now generally identified with the mausoleum of Diocletian forms the present cathedral, the campanile of which caused the destruction of a portion of a peristyle enclosing the mausoleum. This mausoleum is a round building like the Pantheon, and like the latter has a perfectly preserved dome which, unlike that of the Pantheon, was not open at the top. About a quarter of a century ago the interior was restored under the auspices of the ill-matched and ill-fated Rudolf and Stephanie, who are mentioned on a conspicuous tablet, not as furnishing any cash for the enterprise, but as *presentibus et opus admirantibus*. The interior, forty-two feet in diameter, with eight large columns framing four niches and bearing eight smaller columns superimposed, makes a fine impression, although the space seems rather small for a cathedral. A sculptured frieze encircling the dome at the bottom, and containing, among other things, hunting scenes, must be catalogued as "shapeless sculpture."

After being *presens* and *admirans* for half a day, wherever I could enter and climb, I sought out Father Bulich, the director of the museum as well as supervisor of all the archæological interests and undertakings of Spalato and Salona, in order to get him to show me the things that were under lock and key. I found him at his house dickering with some visitors for antiquities, and the last I saw of him, two days later, he was engaged in the same occupation. Nothing could exceed his cordiality and his active help. As soon as he could get rid of his visitors he brought out all the best works on Spalato, some of them loaded with illustrations, and sent them around to my hotel. Unfortunately, I could not get half time, even by sitting up all night, to read any large part of them. Then he took me over three of his five or six small museums with which he has to put up instead of the large one for which he prays as well as labors. But though he has done much to bring order out of the chaos which he found, some luckier man than he will probably be the arranger of the museum of Spalato worthy of the name. Amid much that is common and uninteresting, and yet too good to throw away, are objects of great value and importance. Nearly everything is from Salona. He has catalogued and published nearly two thousand seven hundred inscriptions. Gems are strongly represented, as well as coins and other small objects. Sculpture, aside from some good fragments, is represented mostly by sarcophagi, very few of which rise above mediocrity. It is interesting to see here, as elsewhere, a sarcophagus with the representation of Phædra and Hippolytos spared by the Christians, who took Hippolytos as the "chaste Joseph." The oldest object in any of the museums is a sphinx shown by an inscription to belong to Amenophis III., the Memnon of the Greeks, of about 1500 B.C. In one museum is a cast of a really fine head of Herakles, found in the neighborhood but kept by the monks at Sinj.

Of objects which did *not* come from Salona may be mentioned certain Greek inscriptions which show the presence of Greeks on these coasts and islands long before the great days of Rome. Of course it was unlikely that, having put a girdle of colonies around southern Italy, and pushed up along the eastern shore of the Adriatic as far as Epidauros (Ragusa), they should remain strangers to this region so crowded with islands, just their kind.

Father Bulich took me also into the one building inside the palace that is kept locked. Its chief attraction is a perfectly preserved barrel vault with coffers containing rosettes. This is supposed, partly from its position, to have been Diocletian's court chapel; but whether it was dedicated to Jupiter or to Æsculapius is a question which divides the authorities. Lanza, Bulich's predecessor, inferred from a laurel wreath bound by a ribbon which he took to be the imperial crown, sculptured in the rear gable, that *this* was Diocletian's mausoleum. This rear end was said by the guide-books to be inaccessible, and so of course it was what I most wanted to see. I mentioned my regret, and, to my surprise, Bulich said, "Oh! it is perfectly accessible." Then he led the way through several by-ways and up three flights of stairs, almost tumbling over children in the dim light, until at last we got into a kitchen which was backed up against the gable. There was the laurel wreath, to be sure. Little did it interest the rosy-cheeked woman who had her sleeves rolled up above her elbows and was trying in some embarrassment to get them down again before a stranger. The wreath was out of her reach; but the horizontal cornice of the gable was only about four feet above the floor of her kitchen; and she had deployed upon it—a splendid shelf—her oils and essences, her butter and sugar, and all the appliances of a kitchen and a pantry. When Bulich, with all the authority of an archæologist and a father confessor combined, reproved her for quite a good-sized, fresh nick on the left ascending cornice, her cheeks and even her arms took on a redder hue, probably on account of my presence; for the priest was greeted on every staircase as a familiar friend.

The next day he showed me his excavations at Salona, which he has carried on under great difficulties. Since the Austrian empire has no law for the expropriation of private property for the purpose of archæological excavations, he has been obliged with his not all too generous funds to make his peace with the owners of the fields; and, since the whole area of Salona is covered by one continuous vineyard, it has been very slow business. But he has managed to get a foothold here and there. Here the greater part of a big amphitheatre has been uncovered, here a long line of sarcophagi; at present he is pushing a few yards farther the uncovering of a huge Christian basilica.

There had been no great surprises for me at Spalato; but Salona, which had been to me a mere name, now suddenly loomed large before my vision as the great city of the Occident next to Rome. Three things made Salona what it was. It had in the first place a fine harbor at the end of a deep bay. The silting up of the harbor in modern times has brought it a little farther from the water's edge; but that the water once lapped its walls is shown by its water gate. Secondly, just back of Salona there is a great gap in the long chain of mountains that follow the shore at a little interval as far as the eye can reach. Through this gap a great road led into the heart of the Balkan peninsula through what is now known as Bosnia and Servia to the Danube and beyond. Thirdly, the region back of the gap was vastly important to the Romans as a gold-bearing land. In the times of Augustus and Tiberius gold was commonly referred to by the poets as "Dalmatian ore." Salona was the place where all this gold was gathered for transmission to Rome.

The Romans' greed for gold was here seen in its sharpest phase. They dug miles into the heart of mountains, and carried water hundreds of miles in artificial channels for washing deposits of gold. Perhaps no one can ever convey or even conceive of the horror of the life of slaves in these works. In droves of tens of thousands, many of them made slaves instead of masters by the mere fortune of war, they were driven into the bowels of the earth with poor chance of seeing the light again. It is, at any rate, a fact that months passed without such re-emergence, a fact which lessened the likelihood of any re-emergence at all. In that great and cruel empire, slave life counted for little; the supply was abundant.

Arthur Evans, who has recently given back to us the palace of Minos, made in a series of essays some twenty-five years ago what French savants would call a "most penetrating study" of the roads and mines of Dalmatia and adjacent regions. Realizing from this book the importance of this great highway from Salona, and being already strongly lured by the sight of that great yawning gap in the mountain range, I took advantage of the fact that my appointment with Bulich was not until four o'clock to make the day a day of exploration. Taking an early start, I worked my way up to the top of the pass over a road laid out with such a gentle grade that I was able to bicycle over nine-tenths of the distance. Arrived at the top, I went on by a gentle down grade four or five miles into the interior toward Sinj; but, finding no commanding point of view, I returned to the top of the pass. From this point the view can hardly be overpraised. Exactly in the middle of the deep cut is Clissa, a sharp cone, on the truncated top of which is a strong fortress with a straggling village on the slope facing Spalato. Although there are no evident remains of masonry in the fort earlier than the mediæval period, there can be no doubt that a fortress primeval existed here. For once Baedeker deceived me in saying that admission to the fortress would be granted on presentation of a visiting card. The non-commissioned officer in charge stood by his guns, and, in spite of all importunity, refused admission except on the strength of a written permit from the commandant at Spalato. So I contented myself with a view from a point outside the walls some twenty feet lower down. Since it is mainly the view toward Spalato and the sea that is important, there was practically nothing lost. There was just a little feeling of defeat, of being baffled in an attempt to reach the highest height. A railroad is just now approaching completion from Spalato up through this gap to Sinj. When it is finished visitors can enjoy from its many windings all this fine view at their ease.

CLISSA

In twenty minutes I dropped down to Salona, and devoted the rest of the day to exploring the territory of Spalato westward as far as Traü, its ancient rival. Every foot of this shore is beautiful; but Traü itself surpasses all praise.

Its cathedral, in Romanesque style, is complete and unencumbered with later additions. The great west portal, with the figures of Adam and Eve to the right and left, is held by good judges to be unsurpassed by any other portal, whether Romanesque or Gothic. The campanile alone is Gothic, showing that it was somewhat later. It is to be noted, however, that the transition from Romanesque to Gothic all along this shore was nearly a century later than elsewhere. There are other beautiful churches in Traü, some of them in ruins. In fact, stagnation almost complete has struck the town, which is crowded into a very narrow space on a diminutive island. Its streets are not broad enough for carriages. There is a Venetian loggia near the cathedral, with columns that had seen service elsewhere. Its flat roof has tumbled in and been replaced by a makeshift. There is a fascination in this absolute inertia which contrasts with the growth and activity of Spalato, only twelve miles away in a straight line. Seven or eight centuries ago these two rivals would have torn each other in pieces but for the stern yet, on the whole, beneficent rule of Venice, tokens of which, in the form of the lion of St. Mark, appear all along the coast, but especially in Traü, where they have not been removed. "Traü" is an abridgment of Tugurium, the Roman name of the place; but it had an existence in Greek times, being founded by Syracusan Greeks who came by way of the neighboring island, Lissa. I saw one Greek inscription walled into a house near the landing.

At four o'clock on this day of surfeits I met Bulich at the railroad station, "Salona." He came with a select international party, and for four hours, with tremendous enthusiasm, showed us all about his excavation, and then took us to his excavation quarters, which he calls Villa Tusculum, for a fine supper. I verily believe that had not darkness come on he would have forgotten all about that supper, which was, if not a climax, certainly a fitting close to a memorable day.

A most striking feature of Spalato is the beauty of the women. For some considerable time I had been struck by isolated cases; but one evening, as I sat at a café on the water front where crowds were leisurely passing, I noticed nursery-maids and others of the servant class endowed with beauty which a duchess might sigh for. I have never set much store by statements which make certain cities—Genzano, near Rome, for instance—noted for beautiful women, and so I called myself to a rigid account in this case, and there was no mistaking the cumulative evidence collected in cold blood. To control my own impression I asked Bulich, the aged, the next day whether I was mistaken. "Certainly not," said he, "you are making no new discovery." But, lest he should be considered a prejudiced witness, influenced by local pride, I appeal to the next traveller to look up the matter. He should, however, first prepare his mind by visiting Montenegro.

Knots of men, also, who had come in from the country or from coasting boats, peasantry of the region, men of Slavic race, called here Morlaks, contributed to the picturesqueness of the crowd. Four such men, wearing great red and yellow turbans, jackets covered with embroidery and buttons, great red sashes, and indescribable leg and foot coverings, attracted little attention as they passed and repassed the café where I sat, simply because they were not much more conspicuous than many other similar groups. Transfer some of these groups of men and women to canvas with photographic exactness, color included, and you have Titian. It seems a pity that *"die Kultur die alle Welt beleckt"* should ever reach this sweet corner and reduce all this exuberance of color and form to a dead level. The modern tailor ought not to be allowed to enter here with his profane shears and fashion plates.

Continuing my journey from Spalato, I profited by an hour's stop at Traü to review the cathedral. When we had proceeded two-thirds of the way from Spalato to Sebenico, and had just got into the harbor of Ragonitzka, we were struck by a hurricane which subsequently softened down into a regular "bora," for which Dalmatia is famous. For a few minutes paper parcels and even a pile of books were blown about the deck; but to my surprise certain little red disks on the top of the bare heads of some of the passengers held their places. I then discovered on careful scrutiny that they were held in place by a string carefully concealed in the hair back of the ears. I then made a study of these disks. They merely rested on the top of the head, and could in no sense be regarded as a covering for it. It would be an exaggeration to say that they were no bigger than a ten-cent piece, but not so very much of an exaggeration. To be as exact as possible without actual measurements, I should say that the diameter of most of these was three or four inches. The wearers of them were often clad in an ordinary modern suit of clothes. In Sebenico I continued my comparative study of these red disks. I then found some that nearly covered the top of the head, and at last a few cases that had a slight extension downward all around the head. This made it clear that it was intended for a cap. It furthermore appeared that the more a fellow partook of the nature of a "howling swell" the smaller was his disk. It became perfectly clear, then, that we have in Sebenico a case not of the development but of the disappearance of the cap, what is left being only symbolical, the antithesis of the "tall hat."

We had four or five hours in Sebenico, and I spent most of the time in visiting two great discarded forts on high hills back of the city. It would have been worth while to stop and wait for another steamer in order to make an excursion into the interior; but I had had almost a surfeit of fine views, and kept on my course. Sebenico is one of the strangest of harbors. After heading for it the steamer has to dodge around island after island, and at last, when it seems confronted by a continuous coast line, it finds a little break through which it goes in and finds itself in a broad bay. When one looks back one wonders how he ever got so far inland with a steamer, and how he is ever going to get out again to the sea that looks so far away. From its sheltered situation, Sebenico was for ages a pirates' nest. The hand of Venice was here also needed to keep Sebenico from preying on her neighbors, Traü and Spalato. Now all the jarring states rest quietly in the bosom of Austria, except that the contention between the old Italian civilization and the new and aggressive Slave element grows ever fiercer, with the danger that the Italian element will be crowded to the wall.

In about four hours after leaving Sebenico we were at Zara, which enjoys the double distinction of being the capital of Dalmatia and the home of maraschino. It has several churches of absorbing interest, both for their architecture and for their contents. Although it has lost immensely in picturesqueness by the tearing down of its old walls, it is still a beautiful city; but it is a modern kind of beauty, which has come from broad boulevards taking the place of the landward wall, and a splendid quay taking the place of the sea wall. Austrian officers in fine uniforms set the tone. It has almost too much of an air of thrift to be picturesque. One sees everywhere, signs of maraschino factories, maraschino stores, and maraschino cafés.

As I sat in front of a café on the modern quay, sipping my second glass of maraschino at what claimed to be the original maraschino establishment in the city, and looked off at the eight Austrian war-ships lying off the shore, a feeling of "change from the old to the new" came over me. Just then such a sunset as is rarely vouchsafed to man was transpiring. The blood-red sun of double size was setting in the illumined sea. I took it as a signal that my Dalmatian journey was at an end. Pola and Fiume I already knew, and Trieste was a common mart. I went back to the steamer.

GREECE.

Milton Keynes UK
Ingram Content Group UK Ltd.
UKHW040311181024
449757UK00005B/483